Conceptual Communal Home Design:

The Functional and Efficient, Land-Conscious Way

Christopher John Eldridge

Order this book online at www.trafford.com
or email orders@trafford.com

Most Trafford titles are also available at major online book retailers.

Print information available on the last page.

ISBN: 978-1-4120-1820-3 (sc)

Trafford rev. 07/14/2022

Trafford
PUBLISHING® www.trafford.com
North America & international
toll-free: 844-688-6899 (USA & Canada)
fax: 812 355 4082

Conceptual Communal Home Design:

The Functional and Efficient, Land-Conscious Way

By Christopher John Eldridge

Edited by Joy Matkowski and Darrell Troutman

Introduction

After running away from home three times as a teenager and suffering through homelessness as a result, I became very serious about life and indeed about housing. Seeing the ghettos firsthand and having to occasionally walk all night just to stay warm made for a rather rude awakening to an otherwise middle-class teen. Unfortunately, many people suffer through similar situations. More than a billion people live in shantytowns. Indeed, most people lack basic services, an education, and proper healthcare. Appalled at such hardships and similarly at the environmental devastation also going on in the world, I gradually began designing very functional and ultra-efficient communal homes as a direct and very personal way of trying to make a difference.

Even before my street experiences I was genuinely interested in a more combined and communal way of living. At the age of 14, for example, I proposed that my family and my friend's family should move in together. Although I argued that, *"together we would realize greater financial security, benefit from the mechanical skills of my friend's dad, and enjoy our social get-togethers much more often,"* the idea was quickly rejected as simply being unheard of.

Three years later, faced with the prospects of eventually having to live on my own, I talked about similar arrangements with a couple high school friends. At that time, we thought we'd be friends forever, so it seemed only natural to consider living this way. Although they did not say no directly, they generally avoided the topic and seemed to have no basic interest in the idea at all.

Later, at the age of 20, I managed to obtain a decent job in warehousing and had a small but growing savings account. That's when I began to sketch out such homes as a way to safely invest my earnings. It didn't take long to discover that with just the right multifamily floor plan you <u>could</u> successfully combine the resources of two or more families with adequate privacy. This lead directly to an 18-year effort, which continues to this day, to design such homes for myself and others.

Initially, I started designing multifamily homes in anticipation of one day having children. As my parents did, I wanted to give my children the freedom to stay on at home as long as they needed, so they wouldn't have to work two jobs or seek some ill-advised path to independence. To accomplish this, I increased the width of the hallways to allow people to pass one another comfortably. I made all the bedrooms an equal size and provided each with its own high-capacity wardrobe room. I learned to consolidate plumbing and planned for a larger hot water heater and a multi-line telephone. I made use of the space normally wasted on formal living areas for more important areas that people would spend more time in, such as offices and exercise rooms. I also leaned the importance of walling off individual living areas so that activities in one room would not affect other areas. I fixed all the shortcomings that I myself ran into while living at home with my parents as an adult.

Having established the importance of *functionality* and *the suitability of a design to meet expected living conditions*, I began to see the usefulness of still larger homes that would allow myself and another couple or two to combine our resources and talents. In such a home, the kitchen was outfitted with the best, most fully featured appliances, which couples could split the cost on. I added additional craft and recreational areas to facilitate the close, family-like relationship between friends of this nature, and I made space available to care for an elderly parent after, say, a difficult surgery.

Although the homes I was drawing steadily increased in size, I noticed that the amount of materials needed to construct them was becoming significantly less than what it would take to construct an equivalent number of single-family homes. By accident, I had stumbled on a fundamental design principle known as *economy of scale:* an environmental plus and a cost-saving advantage! Thus was born the communal homes that I have increased in size, functionality, and self-sufficiency ever since.

Potential Benefits:

Although the communal aspect of living together is often thought of as a rudimentary approach to meeting the basic essentials of life, it is, in fact, a more active philosophy. It is based on the simple truth that "anything that can be done, can be done better, with the assistance of others." Instead of being passive and simply accepting to live without what you cannot afford, this active approach brings together the skills and the purchasing power of more people. This enables more diverse tasks to be accomplished, and better, more fully featured products to be purchased. The skills of carpenters, tailors, chefs and mechanics would certainly provide for much higher quality products and more trustworthy services from within the home than what is available out in society.

Living communally can also have far-reaching environmental benefits and offers residents other advantages that they don't normally expect to find:

- Larger multifamily homes are more economical to build than many smaller ones and are more energy efficient to operate. They also save land because it requires fewer roads and driveways to access a single building as opposed to many.

- There is a lessened demand for outside services (such as daycare) and greater home security in a home that has more people around.

- More active residents that are strapped for time will find the mutual support of others an outright blessing. They will come home to fully prepared meals, and they can get out more often on the weekends when they don't have to worry about shopping, mowing the lawn, or taking care of pets.

- Although there would be much less individual privacy in a shared communal home, there is a unique ability for such a home to include numerous enhancements to offset this shortcoming. Home movie theaters and libraries can be added and there is a fully equipped exercise room, a pool table game room, and state-of-the-art computer workstations in all of my designs! Such movie, exercise, and game areas would be great (and more frequently used) when other people of the same age and interests are around to enjoy these types of activities with.

- Sub-industrial-scale wood and metal shops, craft and project areas, offices, waiting and reception areas, and garage bays large enough for work-related vehicles will allow residents of such homes to establish a wide variety of self-supporting home-based businesses. Working from home increases our free time and eliminates the daily impact of traveling on the environment!

- Larger, commercial-quality communal homes last longer and are more structurally stable. When combined with their high capacity and functional internal layout, this makes them better able to cope with an emergency or large-scale natural disaster.

Current State of Communities Nationwide

Although it is customary for college students to share an apartment or dormitory, most people do not normally want to live with other people. People are usually quite emphatic about maintaining their own personal lives. However, there are times when people are forced to share their homes with their children longer than they expected to, with an elderly parent that needs their care, or with other families on account of economic hardships. In Queens, New York, for example, the New York Times noted that:

"A combination of stubborn poverty and a dwindling supply of affordable housing has lead to a surge in illegal apartments, wedged into virtually any available nook or cranny." The article went on to note that there were literally *"thousands of illegal apartments and pockets of mild poverty on otherwise middle-class streets." "Enterprising landlords have sliced one or two family houses into multiple apartments, most often converting attics and basements into makeshift flats."*[1]

In such unplanned situations, people are forced to share a home that was only designed for a single family and thus can suffer greatly from the home's inherent limitations.

Occasionally, families and groups of people do intentionally band together, or at least plan ahead for such situations. In-law suites, which are usually an extra first-floor bedroom built to allow adult children to provide some initial care to an elderly parent, are not uncommon. Some larger, more organized groups of people often choose to build their homes in an organized development with the direct intention of providing some basic support for one another. They organize events, watch after each others' kids, help prepare meals, and take turns caring for a common garden.

An integral part of these communities (often called Co-Housing Developments), which can include dozens of individual homes, is a large, central common house that residents build and share with one another. These common houses (see Appendix A – Common House Problems – on page 114) usually contain a restaurant-quality kitchen and dining area, as well as laundry facilities, activity areas (for conducting group meetings), offices, shops, and children and teen areas, too. Apart from a common house, these communities may also share a common garage area, which can be closer to the main road. This not only saves land, it prevents driveways, garages, and streets from degrading the landscape of the central community and it is generally safer for children.

---

[1] The New York Times – October 18th 1996

Occasionally, still other groups of people form actual communes. Communes share many of the same features and benefits of a Co-Housing development, but the people who live there don't live by themselves in individual homes. Instead, they share their home with one another. These often specifically designed multifamily homes can become quite large, housing 20 to 30 people in some cases. With the exception of personal bedrooms and closets, people share all other areas of the home. These shared living spaces are called common areas. Vehicles may also be shared.

There are usually rules (which are decided upon upfront by everybody) called norms that help govern daily life in such homes. Norms can include washing your hands before going to a common food counter, eating everything you put on your plate, specifications of when it is all right to play the stereo loud, and times when it is not. Occasionally, norms may even govern things like how much (if any) attire is required for short trips to the bathroom in the middle of the night. There may also be hygiene norms to follow.

The largest of these multifamily homes can actually exceed a capacity for several hundred people and can be the size of a modern five- to ten-story office building. Such large structures are hard to label as multifamily homes; thus, I will use the term *multi-residential facilities* instead. By the end of this book, we will have worked our way up to the designs and the myriad of benefits of just such facilities.

Communes and co-housing developments (both of which can be correctly referred to as communities) are often incorporated as nonprofit corporations. Some are religious groups that fit the standard model of a nonprofit organization, and others simply incorporate to avoid over-taxation and to gain other benefits that will help them govern themselves and their resources more carefully. According to the 1995 Communities Directory, more than 33,312 people lived in some 467 communities, of one sort or another, across the country.[2] Although some of the largest communities exceeded 3,000 people, the population usually ranged between 8 and 300 residents. Smaller communities, with up to 20 residents, were obviously much more common, but larger communities, with between, say, 150 to 200 members, had a greater percentage of the population.

Currently, many of these communities are only focused on same-sex or religious orientations. Those that are not specifically typically have populations representative of all walks of life. In very open communities, sexually active residents are free to have more than one partner, homosexual tendencies might be openly expressed, and nudity may not be uncommon. Overall, socially minded folks would certainly find all of the group activities, such as parties, bonfires, card games, yoga and martial arts practices, music, crafts, and the restaurant-style dining environment, very enjoyable!

Another common thread in existing communities seemed to be a trend to a more basic *living simply* lifestyle, which avoids overly excessive amounts of personal belongings as much as possible. Although one community showed movies on the weekend and had plenty of PCs, for example, televisions were restricted and most other things were shared. In some rather extreme cases, communities that wish to maintain a certain level of equality among residents will even prohibit residents from tapping external savings accounts while they are living there. Everyone was treated equally regardless of prior success.

---

[2] The Communities Directory – A Guide to Cooperative Living

Work Opportunities and Self-Sufficiency

Many communities operate one or more full-fledged commercial businesses right on their grounds. This not only leads to greater self-sufficiency and an increased savings for residents, it also provides an opportunity for residents to work right where they live. Such businesses can include commercial production, automotive, retail, and warehousing facilities as well as large-scale farming and gardening operations that can supply most—if not all—of the community's dairy, meat, and vegetable needs. Larger communities may even be able to staff a small medical clinic, eye and dental practices, or offer nursing home care at a tenth the cost of an outside facility. Daycare and home schooling can also be accomplished with increased safety, peace of mind, and a higher quality of education.

On the scale of a community, even the common support functions of cooking, cleaning, and grocery shopping become potential part- and full-time jobs for residents. How best to handle these chores will be discussed in chapter two. Having such wide-ranging activities available for residents right where they live not only helps them to avoid the expense and frustration of traveling to work, but also the monotony of working at a single job year after year.

In other situations, residents may simply pay rent to stay at a community while working at an outside job and going to outside activities. A combination of having one spouse work for an outside employer while the other contributes time directly to the support of the community may be essential in smaller communities. This arrangement would help pay the bills, and it takes full advantage of the medical plan offered by an outside employer to cover both a husband and wife.

Noticeable Issues and Concerns

Although great potential exists for this method of combined living, few people see it as anything much more than a happy-go-lucky social experiment or as just something for fringe groups. Such groups simply gloss over the lack of individual privacy as a small price to pay for their uniting cause. Most people, however, just want to be smarter and more efficient about life, not become members of an extremist group. Even thought better ways of living communally exist, none of the communities I visited ever bothered to tap into the potential of analytical design[3] to derive the high-power performance that middle-class Americans would demand. Instead of incorporating large wardrobe closets in each bedroom, for example, one group had very small bedrooms without any closet space at all, forcing newcomers to sell off or donate all of their belongings. Instead of incorporating large, high-performance, men's and women's bathrooms with fully enclosed toilet stalls and separate shower areas, several groups actually had a shared bathroom policy. They shared an ordinary bathroom between far too many people and seemed absolutely elated about their openness and willingness to use it simultaneously: men, women, and children.

Instead of one or two large buildings with four to six floors and a focused internal layout, the communities I visited had sprawling one- and two-story multi-building arrangements. This arrangement forced each building to have its own kitchen, which led to redundancy, inefficiency, and a substantial amount of clutter. Recreation areas also suffered

---

[3] A careful analysis of needs and the operating environment as a whole to generate more effective and efficient solutions.

from this sprawling layout. Exercise rooms seemed shoddy and halfheartedly equipped and common living rooms seemed vacant a large percentage of the time and rather poorly equipped because there were so many. Surprisingly, there was also not a single pool table game room in any of the places I visited, despite the obviously large number of people that could have enjoyed this feature. To me, several much more fully featured and diversified recreational areas could have been designed into a larger home that combined the resources of all these smaller buildings.

Unfortunately, most new-age initiatives to improve on our way of living are nothing more than half-hearted gestures. Whereas extremist groups go too far in catering only to fringe elements, hybrid communal groups don't go nearly far enough as they wish to have it both ways. They want a-typical private homes in a community of like-minded people but this is incredibly wasteful. Co-housing developments, for example, have a similar duplication of kitchen and living areas as mentioned above, which results in similar problems. Although proper land use was highly touted at one community I visited, I noticed fundamental design flaws throughout, which actually contradicted this guiding principle. For example, not only was this group planning to use an a-typical *one-level* parking lot, they were planning one that was even more wasteful to land than normal. Instead of having one parking lot 'aisle' to drive down, supporting parking slots on both sides, this development planned two parking lots with one aisle and only one side for parking slots each. When I pointed out that both sets of parking slots could be combined in a single parking area with only one aisle, thus eliminating the land use of one entire aisle (which are typically 25 feet wide, and theirs was over 50 feet long), the representative simply glossed over the error. Furthermore, their individual homes all seemed to have cathedral ceilings, which is basically unused volume to have to heat, wasting energy. Their driveway was a quarter-mile longer than it had to be, wasting land. Lastly, their supposed land savings was based against people living in individual homes on large rural lots, not based on the actual land use of rural homes compared with their own homes, which had similar footprints.

Conservation may have been on the lips of those at this particular development, but it certainly wasn't deep in their hearts! In my opinion, this type of conceptually fraudulent image of co-housing and the 1970s-type mentality of present day communes can barely win the hearts of a few thousand people, let alone, the hundreds of thousands, if not millions, it will take to really help improve this world. Before people trade in their wasteful SUVs and private suburban homes for life in a commune, they will have to be assured they are not only getting more for their trade, but the *most* from their efforts!

One of the most deeply rooted problems we face involves just how beset the whole architectural design process is with social and individual interpretations. Typically, architects are out to make a name for themselves and are all too happy to placate to a client's demands for something special and out of the ordinary. This has led to one fancy construction project after the next, with wasteful decorative exteriors, wasteful open interiors, and amazingly low levels of performance. The Taisie Corporation of Japan actually highlighted the fact that one of its office buildings had 60% internal free space. Such a building could have had 60% more performance, 60% less land use, or have been 60% less expensive.[4]

---

[4] Taisie Corporation – 1998 annual report

Potential Solutions

Throughout this book, I focus on the design aspects that not only can make life in a multifamily home completely acceptable for almost anyone, but that can actually increase the quality of living thought to be ideal by middle-class America itself! To do this, we need a home that is more specifically designed for the needs we have now and that reflects all that has changed. So much has changed technologically, socially, and environmentally throughout our society that we can no longer view our homes as just a casual place to sleep and relax, where all we do is decorate them with furnishings and fancy exteriors.

A home is a platform of capabilities! It is a cutting-edge solution intended for us to gain a stronger foothold on our needs while attempting to minimize our negative effect on the environment. The more suitable a design can become to the actual way we live, the more energy it can preserve, and the less we'll have to work for someone else to make ends meet. Instead of having a purely romantic view of the home or using it to portray some sort of ideal, we must turn to the unbiased medium of analytical design to uncover exactly what requirements we should be hoping to satisfy. *Preset requirements,* laid out carefully and at length by the process of design analysis, means too much to our quality of living to be compromised by a desire for aesthetics or the influences of class structure, aspects that limit contemporary homes to the most rudimentary levels of performance to be sure.

Instead of fancy broken rooflines, showcase living areas, and narrow front porches that no one even uses anymore, a concentrated blend of detailed functionality, efficient practices, and high-performance features must be utilized for us to realize our potential and avoid the many serious and troubling situations that can arise in life. Only by splicing together all of the tools that we have at our disposal—to function as a *single* and comprehensive system in a planned and deliberate action of self-enhancement—can we ever hope to achieve an overall balance with nature and a fullness in life!

As an amateur designer, I make absolutely no attempt to be stylish by including fancy exteriors, open or flowing internal areas, or cathedral ceilings. It is this apparent lack of concern for fully utilizing every inch of available space that has greatly contributed to our current environmental dilemma. There is literally so much unused, open space in our society that I often feel crowded out by space itself. My design goal has, thus, been to devise concepts that will eventually use 1/50th of the amount of land that rural and suburban communities use to support themselves. This is how much excess space I think needs to be eliminated from our sprawling shopping centers and homes to rebound from this building environmental holocaust. One-level, ten-acre parking lots, for which the builder simply paved over the land they needed for parking, are everywhere.

Homes, too, have far more space than they actually need. For as many people who like open and flowing living areas, an equal number of people like the consolidated, snug feel of a cozy den. I, myself, prefer the closeness of a layout that is best associated with what you'd find on a small yacht, where everything is consolidated, built-in, and fit perfectly to the contour of the ship's hull. Such well-thought-out, space-conscious arrangements are remarkable in their detail and quality, and stand in sharp contrast to the ungainly look of a contemporary home's bedroom and living areas. It is this customized, built-in approach, which can yield master bedrooms that are 20% smaller with 50% more desk and drawer space, that I am calling for in these ultra-efficient homes of tomorrow!

Although I live very simply as a bachelor living on my own, I *do not* think this is how we should live communally. To me, building the conceptual foundation for multifamily living calls on us to see the similar needs of individual families, not as an outright justification for conservative, simpler designs, but as only the beginning to a far more comprehensive and resourceful system. I believe that using such things as computers and entertainment centers to their fullest is even more conservative than trying to make do with as little as possible because so much more can be accomplished. Capturing the elemental similarities between individual families and harvesting the full potential of technology and teamwork calls for the ***full augmentation*** of the group's individuality, productivity, and sociability. Having many fully featured activity areas in the home, such as an exercise room, art rooms, and home movie theaters, is therefore a vital part of my designs. I feel that well-made belongings (with a hint of luxury that reflects this quality and completeness) and activity areas, which are used only recreationally, are critically important! They lead directly to a greater fullness in life that Americans will demand!

We want to use these attributes in proportion to the number of residents to improve life, not just concentrate it in one location. Although preserving the environment and improving the quality of life may seem like conflicting requirements, they are actually quite possible if we make the most of our technologies and know-how.

To this end, this book offers a wide range of conceptual communal home designs that not only make communal living entirely possible, but truly desirable—even for those few of us out there driving around in his and hers Jaguars.

- In response to the economic and social dilemmas facing our children (who all too often end up on drugs, in abusive porn films, or in a foreign war zone), I will propose three compact, four-, five-, and seven-bedroom extended-family homes that will allow our children to stay on indefinitely. This proposal, and all of the architectural details needed to accomplish this comfortably, is discussed next, as well as how we can alternately use such added bedroom and closet capacity to help friends in need or an elderly parent after a difficult surgery.

- In response to the economic hardships and time constraints being placed on middle-class families, I present three larger multifamily homes that can comfortably accommodate four to ten families for mutual support. Such homes are well equipped with recreation areas and have extensive work and shop areas to permit <u>substantial</u> businesses and private practices to be located right at the home itself. The many benefits of working at home and what living in such a home would be like are discussed in full along with this.

- Last, I will test the theoretical waters by proposing 7- to 21-level facilities that use between 88% to **98% LESS LAND** than an equivalent number of single-family homes and businesses. These are the environmental cornerstones of my work and provide a resounding response to our planet's environmental holocaust! Such buildings would have a complete array of fully featured activity centers such as 140-seat convention centers and rooftop tennis and basketball courts. They would also have sub-industrial-scale shops and offices that give <u>all</u> residents the ability to work more productively right from their own home. Multiple floors greatly magnify the land-saving qualities of communal living and are a must if we are to achieve both a reduction in land use and an actual increase in our quality of living.

As you work your way though this book, you will begin to notice how more and more quality features become possible as the size of these homes increase. Smaller homes often have to compromise in order to fit in what they can, while larger designs soak up one important feature after the next. It is also important to bear in mind that on a fundamental level, no given home design is ever truly complete. They are constantly being refined, improved, and replaced. One could spend hours strategically placing light switches and wall outlets within a home, let alone the actual walls and rooms.

Much like designing a faster circuit or computer chip, further refinements to a home's layout are always possible. We must be just as open to minor improvements as we are ecstatic about each new and compelling leap forward. Old designs simply become the yardsticks to help measure the effectiveness of the new.

Currently, the most recommended home design presented in this book is the six-level, 23-bedroom home **(Figures 23 to 27)** found in chapter four. Called *Concurrence,* it stands as the leading design best able to meet the unique demands of our present-day situation. Having the right design that will meet or exceed our needs and that people will be happy with can help shave decades off our environmental recovery time because such homes would be more widely accepted. For those interested in building such a home, I provide contact information in the back of the book so that you can get caught up on the latest news and developments.

"Homes are lacking their own **'high-definition,'** *not because high technology and logical progression cannot be applied to them, but because* **casual living** *has no measure of performance associated with it to help us gauge how well a home really suits our changing needs."*

Chapter One

Extended-Family Homes

Homes are not a passing fad or an unnecessary luxury. They are a fundamental need, which justifies building them to the highest possible standards and with the most capabilities that we can! Deciding what features should be built into a home, which if built today could last as long as 130 years, is, however, a difficult but necessary task. Economic hardships, natural disasters, and family crises, which do not generally occur over a noticeable span of time, are inevitable over a span of 75 or 100 years, thus warranting a very cautious approach to home designing. Certain other predictions about what else might happen during this span of time must also be made to ensure that the home maintains its ability to support our needs. The development and widespread use of flying cars **(Figure 12 – Page 41)** or in-home computer workstations, for example, could lead us to develop a home that was significantly different than if these advances were thought unlikely. Both flying cars and computer workstations would permit us to take and maintain a job much farther away from home than is now possible. This would decrease the need to keep moving from one location to the next, so that we could always be near where our jobs were.

Without the fear of always having to relocate, couples could select or build a home that was more to their liking and needs, rather than a rubber-stamped, three-bedroom, beige-carpeted home that could be sold more quickly. If, for some reason, you wanted a five-car garage, purple carpeting, or more functional built-in furnishings, you wouldn't have to worry so much about getting your investment back when it was time to sell. ***Committing to a place to live*** in this way has very profound implications on how much we can ultimately achieve with a home design and, therefore, how much we can ultimately get out of life.

The home itself is a grouping of features that a family depends upon. Like the many organs of the human body, a family's need to live and function forces the integral components of a home to act as a complete system. If while focusing on the home's appearance, for example, one of these integral components gets misplaced or thrown out as something thought unnecessary in the haste of planning, then, throughout the entire life of the home, things will have to be done to compensate for this error. An inadequate hot water heater, a poorly arranged kitchen, or the absence of a home office are examples of oversights that can force residents to work around this shortcoming on a daily basis.

The absence of an office, for example, forces people to use many other areas of the home to put office-related items. When I counted up the number of places where my mother had her papers, books, receipts, and so on, it totaled 24 different drawers, kitchen bowls, countertops, and closet shelves throughout the home. These places were not intended for these purposes and only served to scatter potentially important documents and owner's manuals that were then nearly impossible to find when she needed them. Complete systems that can adequately handle the situations we can expect to face during the life of the home can, in this sense (much like the body), be thought of as a package deal!

By definition, systems round together all of the features necessary to secure the smooth flow of operations throughout the life of the home, day after day and year after year. Adverse fluctuations, even if they don't generally happen to everyone, must be decisively confronted. Allowing deviations in a home's performance to occur at critical times is an irresponsible gamble. American middle-class families, for example, build their homes around a rather unrealistic storybook life. In it, they see themselves as having a couple of kids, who they send off to college at the age of 18, and who, after graduating into good jobs and a successful marriage, leave home to live successful and independent lives. Rarely do the parents consider the possibility that their child may have to stay home longer because of low wages or return home as a young adult, perhaps even as a young parent. They go on the presumption that the economy will remain stable and have even chosen to dedicate significant portions of their home to showcase-like second formal dining and living areas that are seldom ever even used. Thus, when a child moves back in because of a divorce or the loss of a job, these contemporary homes, claimed to be designed for comfortable family living, suddenly become insufficient.

Homes are intended to raise children. So why not go the extra distance to provide them with the privacy and closet space they will need as adults? Being able to afford our children some extra time at home so they can get on their feet and avoid high indebtedness can make a world of difference to them. It may, in fact, be our only way of helping them avoid having to cope with a meager existence, an abusive spouse, or a demeaning, backbreaking, or outright dangerous job.

Extending our responsibility to support our children beyond the age of 18 isn't a bad reflection on us as parents either. I learned firsthand the value of being allowed the time to figure out what my interests were before going off to college. When I did decide to go to college at the age of 26, it wasn't because my parents told me to or because I wanted to "party" and meet girls. It was because I was interested in learning astronomy. Being interested, as opposed to being bored, makes a world of difference in what you learn and how well you learn it. I went from a dropout who despised any and all notions of going to school to maintaining a 3.8 GPA and being asked by my professors to tutor two college-level courses for them (proving to me on a personal level, the truly inspirational value that science has in getting people to want to learn). Remaining at home during college and afterward as a professional programmer has given my mother a modest second income that she can use for retirement. It has also allowed me to save tens of thousands of dollars toward the purchase of my own multifamily home.

One problem with several adults trying to live together in a contemporary single-family home is that it can be like living in an empty barrel, where every sound can be heard in every other part of the home. One needs to do nothing more than drop the toilet seat to have it echo throughout the house. We must ask ourselves, though, is this the fault of the person who dropped the toilet seat? Or is it that contemporary homebuilders have made absolutely no effort to control household noise levels? I've often said that, when I listen, I can actually hear my mother turning the pages of her novel in the room across the hall with both doors shut. Is this privacy, I ask? Should a noisy page-turner be asked to leave home never to "re-turn" again, or do we have to authoritatively demand them to keep it down?

Most of these privacy issues really hinge on the inadequacies of the home, not the people involved, who are just carrying on with their normal daily routines. Rubber toilet seat mounts, cast iron plumbing (used to lower running water noise levels), and **sound deadening insulation** used within the inner walls and floors of the home, are just a few of the things that can be done to lessen any animosity between children and their parents. A larger hot water heater and a multi-line telephone system are other necessities.

Obviously, if an older child is ignorant or unruly, there really is no choice but to give them the boot out the door. Likewise, an abusive parent is definitely someone to get away from. However, in at least neutral situations, where the personalities of residents do not clash, there is an option to arrange the layout of the home to be more tailored to the situation: allowing for more privacy during realistic family living conditions. Bedrooms can be widely separated, more equally sized, and extra closet space can be added, too.

Bedroom Privacy

Bedrooms are an area of the home where the most privacy is required. Teenagers often spend most of their time in their room because their parents almost always occupy the main living area. Typically, however, bedrooms are clustered together at the back end of a narrow hallway. Such arrangements provide little in the way of privacy. Bedrooms are usually divided only by thin, hollow walls, and use only lightweight bedroom doors that are never more than a few inches apart. In such arrangements, even a normal conversation over the phone or with somebody in an opposing bedroom can be disruptive to somebody else trying to sleep or study. I have even been told to turn my stereo down while wearing a set of headphones. Heavy metal music may be great for the soul, but it is absolute hell on other family members!

Instead of having to share a common wall with your teenagers, bedrooms can simply be placed at opposite ends of the house. Interior walls and floors could be made thicker, and they should all be filled with sound-deadening materials. High-density exterior-type doors that have such things as weather stripping and are lockable could also be used on the inside of the home to help lower noise levels. Through such planning, the impact of different lifestyles and work schedules can be minimized. Basically, in small four- and five-bedroom homes **(Figures 01 to 06)** where you want to be able to allow your children to stay on longer or return home if they need to, you can simply modify the home's layout to provide for the necessary levels of privacy. Both of the following homes are also *emergency-enhanced* designs that are better able to cope with regional disasters. Please see Appendix H: Emergency-Enhanced Features on page 128 for those details.

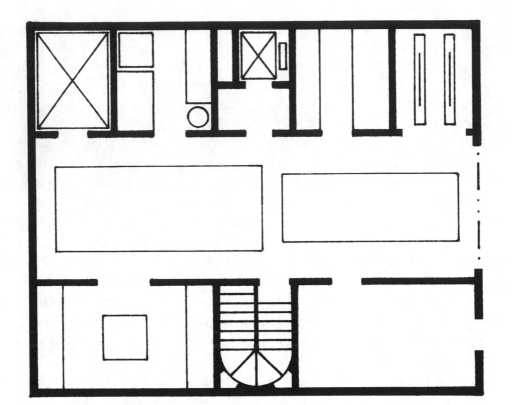

Figure 01 – The Garage Level

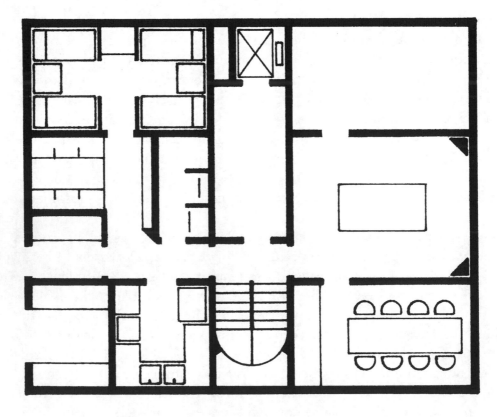

Figure 02 – The Recreation Level

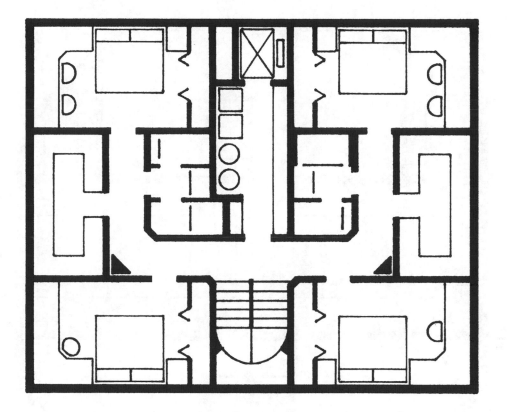

Figure 03 – The Sleeping Level

Figure 01 – The Garage/Basement Level: This functional, 36 x 43.8 (11 x 13.4 m) home has 4,740 square feet overall (including garage and basement). It uses 60% less land than contemporary housing and costs about $470,000. The protective eleven-foot-high central parking area is ideal for a large ambulance-sized work truck and a minivan/SUV. Alternately, three Toyota Echo-sized subcompact cars could be parked in the garage, but there would be only five inches of bumper-to-bumper separation. Upper right is an indented side area for two motorcycles or an ATV.

Across the top are closets for several mountain bikes, as many as ten trashcans, car and home care items, an extra freezer unit, and 75 square feet of bulk storage. Top center is a wheelchair elevator, a ventilation/plumbing shaft, and space for a generator and air compressor. Across the bottom are two 10 x 17.2 (3 x 5.2 m) shops/offices for a small home business, as well as the home's 41-inch-wide (1 m) stairwell.

Figure 02 – The Recreation Level: Upper left is a high-capacity eight-person bunk bed visitors' room sized to help friends in need. Below the visitors' room are a compact six-seat dining booth (wired for laptop computers), a half bath (with urinal and compost toilet, receptacle below), a breezeway exit (lined with equipment racks) that is more secure, an exterior lawn and garden closet, and a 9.2 x 10 (2.8 x 3 m) kitchen. Center is a narrow exercise room (for weights and a treadmill). Right is a 10 x 17.2 (3 x 5.3 m) living room, a 13.8 x 17.2 (4.2 x 5.3 m) pool table/game room, and an eight-seat craft/conference/home schooling classroom. All living areas are separated for enhanced privacy and energy efficiency.

Figure 03 – The Sleeping Level: Four equally-sized 10 x 15 (3 x 4.6 m) master bedrooms can be seen in each of the four corners of this floor. Each has a 13-foot-long desk, a 10-foot-long closet, and allowances for a king-size bed. Two additional wardrobe rooms (left and right center) help further separate these bedrooms and are shared as needed. To fully consolidate the home's plumbing, the laundry room (center, with two hot water heaters) is directly between the home's two full bathrooms. Bathrooms are partially divided for simultaneous use by husband and wife. The design and placement of the stairwell allows easy access to the attic storeroom/greenhouse and a small rooftop patio area.

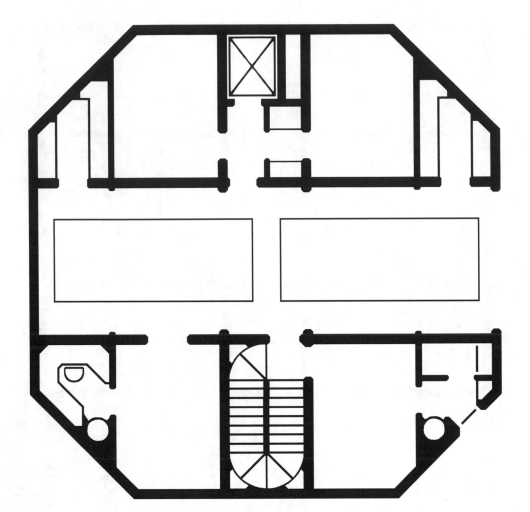

Figure 04 – Level 1 (Partial Basement/Garage):

Running across the center of this next design is a 14.8 x 46.1 central garage bay shown with two 8 x 20 work trucks. Three 14.8-foot-long vehicles are possible but with only six inches of bumper-to-bumper separation. To add flexibility, the bay is 14 feet high. This allows it to hold very large semis, busses, or construction equipment. It can be used for light manufacturing or storage. It can serve as a hangar for small helicopters and it even has ***elevating rafter platforms*** so that if the vehicles below are not very tall, the rafters will be able to store small boats, canoes, ATVs, mountain bikes, and even other cars!

Right of the bottom stairwell is a 10.5 x 14.6 multi-purpose office for home businesses. Right of the office is a double-door entryway with a half bath for convenience. The circular area just below the half bath is a fire pole escape shaft that allows residents to escape to an exit from upper floors more quickly. Since both the office and entryway are only 7.5 feet high, there can be a substantial 5.9-foot-high storage area above them as well! Left of the stairwell is a modest shop with a side workbench room that helps to keep the workbench area separated from all the fumes, sparks, and dust generated in the shop. The stairwell itself is 43 inches wide (on both sides), requires 22 steps to reach level two (24 are possible), and has bulk storage space underneath.

At the top of the design is another office and shop. Between them are an elevator and vent/plumbing shaft, a small kitchenette, and coat rack. Flanking the shop on the right is a storage closet for trash, recyclables, driveway support items, an emergency generator, and an air compressor. Flanking the office on the left is a storage closet for work vehicle support and automotive supplies.

The Skipping Stone Five-Bedroom, Ultra-Emergency-Enhanced Home Design (Figures 04 to 06)

Skipping Stone is a very robust emergency-enhanced home design. Its Octagonal shape not only has 8% to 12% less external surface area than a square or rectangular design (leading to energy and material efficiency), it's far less wind resistant and far stronger when coping with the shockwaves generated by an earthquake or a nearby bomb blast.

The home's 10-inch-thick outer walls are not only stronger due to their shape, they are fully braced from the inside with 10-inch-thick structural support walls. These concrete-filled structural walls—used instead of Tinker-Toy-like I-beam construction—provide maximum support against lateral shockwaves traveling through the ground and can be clearly seen running up through each level of the design. The consistent placement of these walls on each floor adds overall strength and stability to the building. These walls also form a protected inner core—like a building within a building—so that damage to an outer wall won't affect the whole facility.

This design is also very compact—only 28% larger than the previous four-bedroom design—and yet offers 75% more shop and office space, which adds greatly to the home's level of self-sufficiency. Overall, the home is 47.2 feet wide and has a footprint of 2,011 square feet. There are 6,036 square feet in the home overall, which would coast about $680,000. Apart from the five bedrooms, there are five half baths, two completely separate shower rooms, and one regular full bath. The average walking distance from the bedrooms to a half bath is 13.5 feet and the average distance from a bedroom to the stairwell is 30.2 feet.

Unique for such a small design is the very high garage bay with elevating rafter platforms for tremendous extra storage. These elevating rafter platforms can raise or lower depending on how much clearance is needed for the vehicles below, but they don't come all the way down to the bay floor. To get extra cars and other items up to them, there is a large vehicle-sized elevating platform just outside of the garage entrance that can be driven over when it's flush with the ground. This open scissor-lift platform can extend all the way up to level two where cars can even park on a terrace-like platform that can extend out over the entire driveway in some configurations.

Alternative Functions: The National Guard *'Defense Base'* Concept

Because the design is so robust, this home has the potential of serving as a firehouse, police station, or as a National Guard outpost that can have pre-positioned supplies, vehicles, and 24 soldiers per base near most cities. This latter *defense base* concept would allow the National Guard to respond much faster to natural disasters or to various forms of terrorist attacks, which may include an outright assault by dozens of gunmen using guerrilla tactics.

If used by the National Guard, the rooftop of this small facility would have an armored 120mm mortar position, an anti-aircraft ability to confront a hijacked aircraft, a hangar for a small VTOL reconnaissance drone, and a helicopter landing pad. There would be a lot-side waiting room, guard posts, extra fuel under the driveway, and three-quarter-inch steel applied to the outer walls. The garage bay (which protects vehicles by being partially underground and in the center of the design) is ideally sized for large military vehicles and fire engines. Typically, the garage would hold two armored/amphibious 4 x 4 jeeps or vans that can be used in hurricane-force winds, high floodwaters, for entering contaminated areas after a dirty bomb attack, or for when confronting a heavily armed gunman in support of local police units.

Figure 05 – Level 2 (Living):

Center right is a large 14.8 x 18.5 pool table game room with a state-of-the-art audio-video system and a pool table that can retract semi-automatically into the floor between floor joists. On the left side of this room is a 10.7-foot-long dining bar with four bar stools per side. The exit seen on the left leads out to a small terrace located over the entrance to the garage. Above the pool table game room is the home's 10.5 x 14.6 den-size living room. To access the living room, residents simply walk through a hardwood shelving/home office area to the right, which has a phone, PC workstation, printer, safe, and other office and living area supplies. Since there are two doors separating the living room and game room, this shelving/office area can serve as a partial phone booth as well as a sound buffer. Located below the game room is an eight-seat craft/conference room with a library for 1,576 one-inch-thick volumes and a closet for arts and craft supplies.

The home's 9.3 x 10.5 kitchen (left of center) is ideally located for easy access. Along the hall directly below the kitchen is a 16-inch-deep floor-to-ceiling shelving unit that can serve as a pantry, a movie and music library, gun case, and collectable display. Left of the stairs is a 10.5 x 14.6 bunk bed visitors' bedroom with six bottom-entry full-size bunks for up to 12 people. Just below the breezeway rear exit (which is center left) is a shelving area leading to the visitors' room. This shelving area (which helps support people working out back) has a sink, phone, a PC workstation, and some storage space for visitors. Above the breezeway exit is a half bathroom with a composting toilet. Above the half bath are two lawn support closets for garden tools and a riding mower. If the property is not sloped enough to come up this high in the back of the house, these lawn closets can be in the 5.9-foot-high storage space just above the work vehicle support closet and office on level one. Left of the elevator is one of the home's five bedrooms. Just below the elevator is a half bath.

Figure 06 – Level 3 (Bedroom):

On this level you can see four 10.5 x 14.6 bedrooms flanking the stairs at the bottom and the elevator at the top. These bedrooms are just large enough for a king-sized bed, a work desk facing the windows, an entertainment center, and a built-in, wall-to-wall shelving unit for storage. Each bedroom (which are as widely separated as possible) has a unique double-door side entryway that makes them even more private as it creates a further sound buffer. These side entryways contain ample hardwood shelving units and even a small vanity sink where couples can consolidate their personal items and conduct their morning routine without taking up the main bathrooms.

In times of crisis, each of these bedrooms can be converted into a unique bunk bedroom for six to 12 people. As seen in the two bedrooms flanking the stairs, these bunks are situated side-by-side but are fully walled off from one another and only open at the bottom where there is a privacy curtain. These bunks are fully finished inside with things like a small TV angled down from the ceiling, padded armrests with cup holders, and even a stereo/alarm clock! There is also a foldout table and hookups for a laptop. Such unique bunk beds are known as 'capsule bedrooms' and are common in Japanese hotels. There can be up to eight single bunks or six full-sized bunks.

Running across the center of the design is an array of bathrooms and a 10.7 x 13.8 central exercise/laundry room. On either end are a half bathroom (with an additional urinal and diaper changing table) and a completely separate shower room with an ADA-compliant bathtub. The separation of shower rooms and the half baths allows for simultaneously use without loss of privacy. Inward of the left most bathrooms is a regular full bathroom. The central exercise room also serves on one end as the laundry room. Four water heaters can be seen up by the elevator entrance.

Depending on funds, residents can opt to start with just a flat rooftop above, but can then add bulk storage areas, a year-round greenhouse, rooftop patio, and even a small hangar for future flying cars as more funding becomes available.

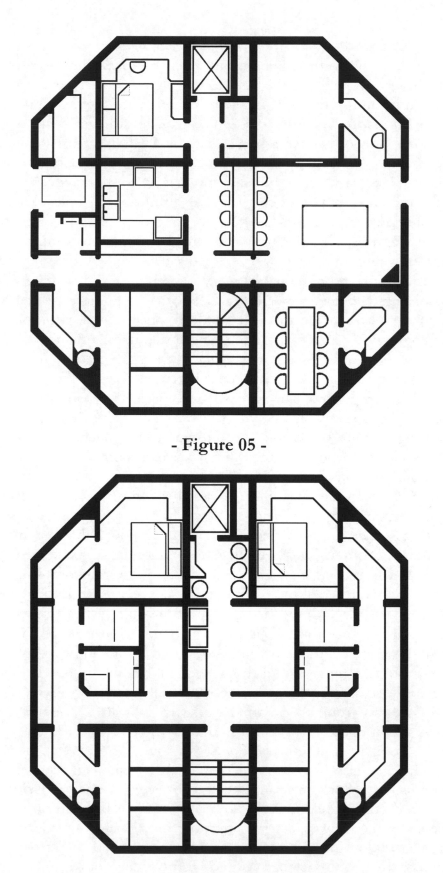

- Figure 05 -

- Figure 06 -

Having the Necessary Amount of Storage Space

Instead of a second formal dining room, a second formal living room, or one extra-large master bedroom, we can use the equivalent volume of these extravagances to make each bedroom a more appropriate size and to provide each of them with the equivalent of a high-capacity, *two-person wardrobe room.* Adequate storage is an absolutely critical aspect of any home, not to mention a home that you are trying to share with other adults! Closet storage is measurable, not by the volume of the closet, but by the amount of wall along which we can hang clothing or put shelving against. Although everyone is different, it usually takes about 26 feet (8.0 m) of closet wall length for two people: about the equivalent of wall length found in a large 8 x 11 (2.4 x 3.4 m) wardrobe room. We benefit from having large amounts of closet wall length because we are able to put such things as the bedroom dresser and armoire into the closet (or, alternatively building in floor-to-ceiling shelving units). This makes more room available in the bedrooms for such things as comfortable chairs, a complete entertainment center, and a desk with a computer workstation.

Adequate personal storage areas are needed to help couples consolidate all of their personal belongings, which are all too often found boxed up in a damp basement, taking up the hallway and living room closets, or hanging in the spare bedroom closet, which now must remain free solely for use by the older children. Basically, the more we are able to consolidate our belongings into our own personal areas, the smoother living with other people will be. A small vanity sink could even be added to some wardrobe areas for use during the morning routines of shaving and brushing teeth. Such an added vanity can free up the use of the main bathroom so much that fewer bathrooms become necessary, and less conflict arises about how long each person uses them.

Substantial closet storage length can be designed into the home in several ways. With only minor modifications, larger bedroom-sized wardrobe rooms, as large as 9 x 12 (2.8 x 3.7 m), can be used as other rooms if needed. This exceptional ability is made possible by providing a wardrobe room with its own separate entrance, just outside the room (or rooms) that it is intended to serve (as we just saw in figure 3). Ordinarily, what these separate entrances leading to two different rooms would do is prevent the differing work schedule of one spouse from interfering with the restful sleep of the other, when they went to change in the wardrobe room and get things out of the closet. However, given the size of the wardrobe room, this also creates the potential for the bedroom and wardrobe room to serve as separate guest rooms, a nursery, or as boys' and girls' rooms if needed. The fact that the wardrobe rooms are so large and can be accessed separately also allows them to remain useful as offices, exercise rooms, or craft areas if your kids are successful enough to move off on their own: far more useful than a formal dining room or formal living room would be.

Wardrobe rooms work especially well as sound buffers when placed between bedrooms, and they can also be used much like a muffler on a car, separating the bedroom from a common hallway. Such an arrangement, with the wardrobe room sitting between the hallway and the bedroom, would not only lower the amount of bedroom noise that can be heard by someone in the hallway, but it's also more functional. Consider that once you are done sleeping, you seldom need to go back to your actual bed to get something that you need. In contrast, when I am getting ready to head out the door in the morning, I always find myself having to run back to my closet to grab something that I forgot. Having the wardrobe room out in front of the bedroom makes these trips back and forth to your bedroom closet that much quicker and that much less distracting to those still trying to sleep. As an entrance to your bedroom, the wardrobe room would be kept more attractive and less cluttered by eliminating such things as those cheap wire rack closet organizers in favor of built-in, floor-to-ceiling cabinetry, which allows boxes on the top shelf and shoes on the floor to be nicely concealed behind cabinet doors.

Instead of overly large wardrobe rooms, it's certainly possible to line some of the hallways leading back to the home's bedrooms with shelving, cabinet, and clothing racks as we saw in the last five bedroom home. This arrangement allows people to manipulate the amount of closet space they use by shifting the belongings of one couple, who may need more storage space, into the area of another couple that doesn't require quite as much. This helps balance out what would otherwise be two static bedroom closets where one becomes almost impassable from holding too many things while the other sits half empty. In such an arrangement, there would still be plenty of storage space available in the individual bedrooms for more personal or valuable items.

In some of my newer designs, I've placed about 24 feet of cabinetry and floor-to-ceiling shelving units in the bedrooms themselves. Such units line about half of the bedroom's walls and would blend in nicely with the built-in desk area and entertainment center. This arrangement allows couples to keep all of their belongings personal and more secure. In my view, it also makes the bedroom more attractive. Whatever storage arrangement you choose will depend on what you are trying to accomplish with the design.

When home designs are pressed for space, adequate closet storage is unfortunately one of the first things to get crossed off the list. Thankfully, we can store things almost anywhere, and we are limited only by our creativity and our willingness to customize our furnishings. Instead of having a box spring under your mattress, you can have a platform bed with built-in drawers. You could create a lower false ceiling over a bed for use as a huge shelf. Bedroom nightstands can be replaced with floor-to-ceiling units offering four times as much storage. There is potential for in-floor storage between the thick steel floor joists. We can store things in the staircase by using step plates that hinge up.

To make the hallways in the home more useful, we could line them with 1-foot-deep (30 cm) shelving units for displaying books, movies, music CDs, and collectables. Overhead storage compartments like those on airplanes can be placed throughout the home: over the living room couch, over the toilet, and in the dining room. Conversion closets are yet another option. These closets contain items that are intended to be swapped out with items in an existing room. A game room pool table, for example, can be swapped out with an air-hockey unit stored in an adjacent conversion closet. We could even add an entire additional level to the home just for storage if we needed to. Without adequate storage, single-family homes could never hope to fully utilize their bedroom capacity.

Creating a Larger Extended-Family Home

When children stay on with parents into adulthood, the workload on a contemporary home is about twice that for which it was designed. Storage quickly becomes a problem, and residents begin to notice how narrow the hallways are, how much noise carries, and just how little two different generations have in common as they battle for the use of the home's only undivided living, dining, and kitchen area. Walling off this main living area into three separate rooms, separating the bedrooms as widely as possible, and providing each bedroom with a large amount of storage space would allow a home to be much more functional and private under these conditions. However, even these higher performance homes can become overburdened depending on the number of children and in-laws that are present. This is especially true during times of economic hardships and natural disasters. Such potential scenarios can be accommodated by still larger home designs that have more bedrooms, but one thing we need to realize before we just start introducing more features and making the home larger, is that even an average home already possesses some of the qualities that it would need to function under such intensified conditions.

Modern homes fall just short of achieving the overall potential that has already been built into them. For example, a modern kitchen, which can far outperform the family kitchens of the 1940s (which used iceboxes and coal-fired stoves to serve up to a dozen children in some families), can support a substantially higher degree of usage than providing merely one main meal a day for three or four people. An average home's two bathrooms are generally as many as most restaurants and offices provide for the large number of patrons and employees that visit them during the day. They are certainly more convenient than the outhouses used by more than half of America just 50 years ago. Another example is that of the home itself. The durability of a home's structure, foundation, and its modern weather-resistant exterior enable even a contemporary home to last as long as 130 years. Current improvements in frame and foundation materials can give a home an almost permanent quality, enabling it to extend its life considerably and weather some of the strongest hurricane-like conditions along the way.

Ultimately, this long-term durability translates into great potential in that any feature that you can afford to add to the home initially will endure to benefit the daily lives and increase the capabilities of every resident. The positive and cumulative effects of these features, which are carried forth for the life of the home, are, however, vastly under utilized by today's residents, who see their homes only as casual places to rest, sleep, and eat after a day's work. Casual living has no measure of performance associated with it. Thus, the improper placement of a bathroom or the misplacement of things that over time add up to thousands of extra footsteps tends to go unnoticed. If written down, nearly any design can meet these three requirements of resting, sleeping, and eating within a causal atmosphere, including a cabin tent or a one-room apartment. To exert so much expense just to meet the basic demands of what essentially amounts to only a few people undercuts the true potential of a vastly more capable structure.

Building single-family homes with such negligible levels of performance reflects just how much our society has been geared to working for "Corporate America:" a vision that is gradually being challenged by lesser paying jobs and which should be considered exceptionally dangerous in lieu of how vulnerable a service economy is to technological advancement. Home efficiency also becomes critically important in homes that are able to last greater spans of time because of the tremendous savings that can be realized over the entire life of the home. The untapped potential that the home already has to offer, especially when laid out functionally, is nearly the equivalent of another separate home. Without having to expand the kitchen, game, exercise, or utility rooms or having to greatly expand the dining room or the number of full bathrooms, a typical home could more than *double* its residential capacity and still function adequately.

It's always possible to upscale a home in incremental steps as long as you are willing to meet the increased demands that will be placed on it. With more dynamic and more important inter-relationships existing between all of the individual components of a larger home, however, it is easy to lose track of what the home really needs to accomplish. You may even end up worse off for your efforts because you'll be tempted to add back an oversized master bedroom, a formal dining room, or a fancy entryway that just aren't necessary. To accommodate double the normal number of residents requires us to take some fundamental measurements to determine what parts of the system are underutilized or overstressed, and at what level of performance these latter features should be expanded to, so that they achieve proportionality with the rest of the system. It also involves coming to terms with what really needs to be done to secure comfortable family living over the long term. For example, things like bulk storage closets (used for excess furnishings) become vital so that the people you offer your home to don't have to sell off all of their own belongings before being able to move in.

A Four-Generation Home Design

A seven-bedroom home **(Figures 07 to 10)**, expanded in size so that <u>each</u> bedroom has the equivalent of a two-person wardrobe room, would be a great example of a home able to suffice in most of the conventional situations modern families are facing. This home could provide comfortable living conditions for you, your children, and your grandchildren, even if everyone involved had a partner living on! You could, alternately, help friends and families in need while renting out a room or two to people you know and trust. Such diverse abilities are quite phenomenal!

With wider handicap-accessible bathrooms, a small wheelchair elevator, and bedrooms that have a 220-volt outlet (to support medical equipment), you would also be able to take care of elderly parents for extended periods. I feel that homes last far too long to forgo such planning. Such disability-related features (which you might need yourself one day) could easily pay for themselves. It may surprise you, but just two years of nursing home expenses could exceed $100,000! Forgoing formalized living areas helps to make many such things possible. It also makes far more sense to invest your money in a good home, rather than in a luxury, sport, or sport utility vehicle that isn't needed!

Apart from serving as a fail-safe to ensure the well-being of loved ones, this type of home could allow up to six or seven young couples to combine their buying power and share expenses. Although most working couples can afford a home or an apartment of their own, they are often forced to live paycheck to paycheck and make purchases on credit. Instead of buying a home that is more than they need (in hopes of growing into it), couples can take a few extra years up front to save their money and develop their job skills. When each individual puts forth a concerted effort to make things work, such a home could provide a far greater standard of living than what each couple could have attained on their own.

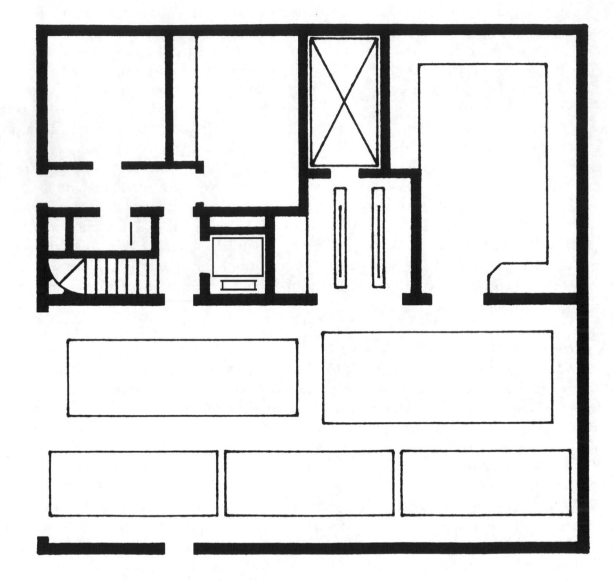

Figure 07 – Level 1 (Partial Basement):

This four-level, 7-bedroom, 45.8 x 47.9 home has 8,766 square feet overall and uses 75% less land than an equivalent number of single-family homes. It would cost about $960,000.

Upper right is a large 15 x 22.6 shop. The garage (bottom) is shown with a minivan/SUV, three Honda Civic-size vehicles, and one ambulance-size work truck. Bumper-to-bumper separation is a minimum of eight inches and side-to-side separation is a minimum of 28 inches. A small side bay adjoining the garage (center) can hold two motorcycles or an ATV. The home's elevator and vent shaft are directly to the left of this motorcycle parking area. Upper left are two easy-to-access 10.5 x 11 and 10 x 15 business offices. Center left is the home's forward stairwell and a small half bath under a portion of it that is capable of incorporating a compost toilet and urinal. In all, there are seven toilets, seven bathroom sinks, one urinal, and three ADA-compliant stall showers in the home. Residents can access the stairs, elevator, and bathroom without having to enter either of the two offices. The stairwells and hallways throughout the home are a minimum of 41 inches wide.

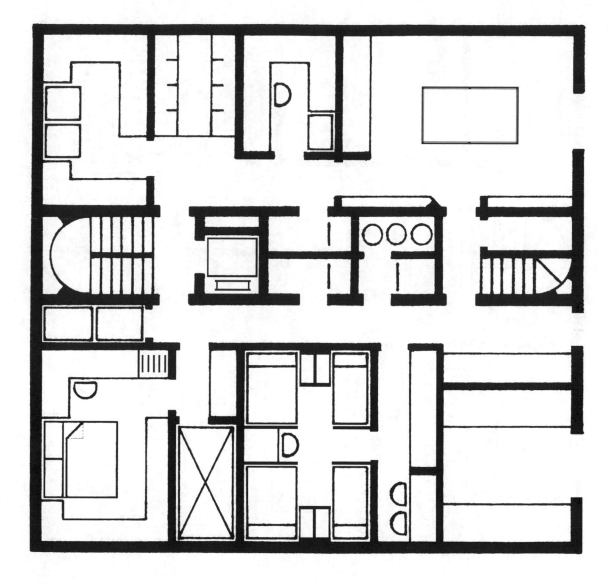

Figure 08 – Level 2:

Upper left is the home's 9.2 x 15 kitchen, which has two refrigerators and a five-burner stovetop. Top center is an eight-seat dining booth (with wall-mounted television) and an 8.2 x 10.3 office that has a large fireproof safe, a computer server, and other shared electronics. Upper right is a 15 x 20 pool table game room that includes a full entertainment center and enough library shelving space for 1,200 volumes.

Lower left is one of the home's seven 11.2 x 16.7 master bedroom suites. Bottom center is a 12-person bunk bed visitors' room with four single bunks and four full-size bunks. Just outside of the visitors' room are shelving units and two PC workstations (where visitors can talk on the phone). Lower right is a ground-level lawn and garden closet and an 11-foot-long breezeway rear exit. This back exit is lined with gear racks and bench seats. Center right is the home's second stairwell with storage under a portion of it. In the center of the drawing are two half bathrooms, a separate ADA-compliant shower room, and three oversized hot water heaters that are very close to the showers.

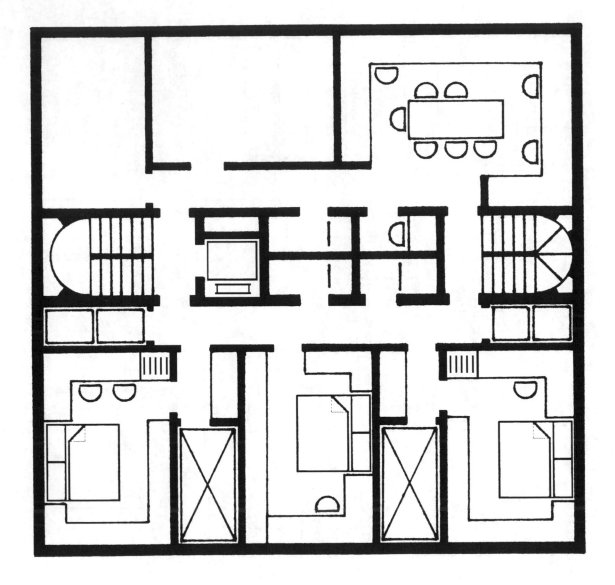

Figure 09 – Level 3:

Running across the bottom of the drawing are three master bedrooms. Each bedroom is shown with a king-size bed and an 11-foot-long desk area for PC workstations and an entertainment center. They also contain 24 feet of cabinet, drawer, and clothing storage racks. The doorway to each bedroom is located away from the corners of the room to help maximize the amount of internal wall length available to place furniture against. Having only one doorway per bedroom also increases the amount of usable wall length. The two corner bedrooms each have a unique double-door side entryway that increases privacy. A bulk storage closet is also used to separate the bedrooms. In the center of the drawing are two half baths and a separate shower room.

Running across the top is a 9.2 x 15 exercise/weight room, an 11 x 16 living room, and a ten-seat 15 x 20.2 craft and home schooling conference room, which contains ample storage shelving for all sorts of hobbies and activities. There is also a sit-down phone booth with a writing desk just below it to increase privacy in both the conference and living rooms.

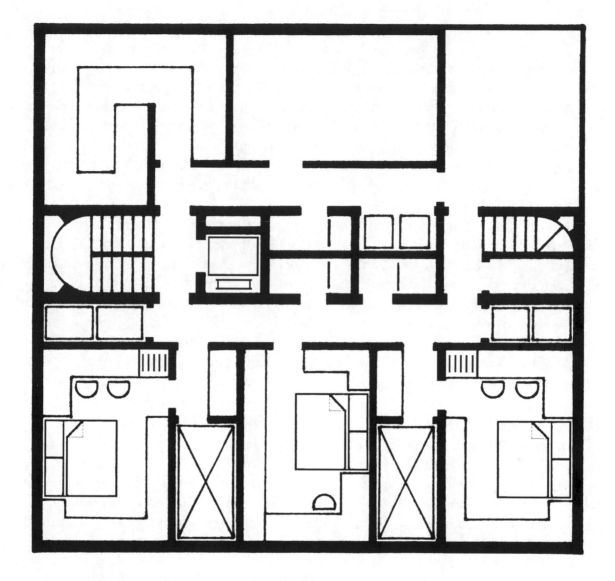

Figure 10 – Level 4:

Across the bottom are three additional master bedroom suites. Apart from adding privacy, the double-door side entryway also has a small shelving and vanity area where couples can carry out some of their morning routines without disturbing those still sleeping. No bedroom in the home borders a bathroom, stairwell, or elevator and they are not above (or below) noisy activity areas.

Upper left is a small greenhouse that provides **38 square feet** of growing area per resident. Top center is the home's main 11.2 x 18 living room, which is far more private than conventional living rooms because it doesn't border a dining room or kitchen and it does not have the distractions of a front door to contend with. In the center—below the living room—is a half bath and a laundry closet. Having the laundry closet on one of the main sleeping levels (as opposed to the basement) is ideal in that it is where most of the laundry actually comes from. Upper right is a large terrace.

The home's five bulk storage rooms provide each bedroom with an average of **61 square feet of storage space**. Above this level is a flat rooftop where flying cars can potentially land.

Instead of having to purchase baseline appliances and electronics, which each couple would then have to live with for years until they wore out, residents could combine their buying power to purchase top-of-the-line models that would benefit everyone. One couple could purchase a top-end, 26-cubic-foot, side-by-side refrigerator-freezer, while others split the purchase of the washer and dryer (ones able to hold up under such workloads) and advanced entertainment systems. Starting off with a better standard of living, greater home security, and a few extra friends is something that, I think, modern couples can really use. After one or two couples establish themselves enough to move off on their own, the remaining couples would be able to think of having children. Living together would enable them to avoid daycare services and all of the travel and time involved with dropping the kids off and picking them up.

Two or three single-parent families, in which the child or children may already be older, could also benefit from the mutual economic support of one another. Today, single parents raise some 31% of all children.[5] If families are breaking up, then a more appropriate home design intended to combine the resources of several split families is the key, not trying to force people to live together via more restrictive divorce laws. Instead of being forced to move back home or waste money renting, it should be possible to find another single-parent family or single who is willing to share expenses. Two or three parents of the same sex could approach their situation with a much more adult attitude and would be the least likely of anyone to develop animosity between one another because of their mutual situation.

Building on the Foundation of Extended-Family Living

In the first four-bedroom home, we gained the ability to help our children while they were trying to establish themselves in our nation's unforgiving job market. In the last seven-bedroom extended-family home, we focused on expanding the home's inherent qualities to give couples or split families more alternatives. Our own children also had the freedom to stay on permanently (even with a family of their own) if they wanted to or needed to. Such arrangements can be mutually supportive financially and can provide a rewarding sense of family and friendship.

These extended-family homes are not the end of such potential. The foundation they established with enhanced privacy and adequate closet space can continue to be used in larger homes that are much more self-sufficient and fully featured.[6] In larger homes, however, we'd not only need larger kitchens and more bathrooms, but things like more extensive shop and project areas that take advantage of what essentially amounts to a small workforce under one roof. If we could work effectively from our own home, at least some of us wouldn't have to waste our time traveling to work in order to work for things that we could otherwise be making for ourselves. We would greatly lessen our impact on the environment through less travel in the process! For these reasons, I believe the draw to the upper performance levels found in a true communal home is undeniable.

---

[5] N.C.R radio broadcast September 18th, 1994

[6] Living efficiently and SELF-SUFFICIENTLY at a very local level are the absolute keys to coping with nearly any type of disaster, economic collapse, pandemic, asteroid impact, or terror attack you can think of. The more we can do for ourselves in times of crises the better off we will be.

Chapter Two

The Analytical Foundation for Communal Homes

The basic needs and day-to-day lives of each individual requires us to seek the shelter and facilities of a residential dwelling. Across the board, the needs of each family and person are nearly identical. Everyone needs a place to sleep, to eat and prepare food, a place to enjoy entertainment, a place to store things, and bathrooms. Similarly, from one household to the next, we are duplicating the same domestic chores as one another. Everyone needs to cook and clean, care for the lawn, and shop for food. Laundry needs to be done, expenses need to be paid, and (to afford it all) some form of work needs to be performed. To someone like myself, who lives alone, these endless domestic chores can take up time I just don't have. I can only imagine what working parents must go through.

In Western society, every business, family, and person seems to be ***ideologically isolated*** (as if by some invisible wall) and forced to go about all of these activities on an individual family-by-family/person-by-person basis. If our needs and chores are the same, then it should be obvious—on a fundamental design level—that they should be combined or at least restructured into whatever new type of home offers residents the most efficiency and benefit. As the most numerous and fundamental part of any community, our homes need to be so carefully tailored and balanced to their leading role within society that these overlaps and duplicated efforts vanish without a trace.

The Efficiency of Increased Size

Economy of scale is a fundamental design principle that directs us to the use of larger designs, which are less expensive, more efficient, and more complete and fully featured. A win – win – win scenario! Apartment buildings, for example, are less expensive per unit to build than individual homes because each one shares a common structural wall. Even using just this simple example, only one step above that of individual homes, building materials are reduced by about 11%. This side-by-side placement also serves to better insulate each unit by lowering the amount of surface area that each has exposed to the elements. This makes them more efficient to heat in the winter and cool in the summer. My mom's townhouse **(Figure 11)**, which sits between two other units, literally has half the electric bills of her previous home. This two-level, middle unit has 48% less surface area exposed to the elements compared to the one-level ranch she had! The entire four-unit building she lives in has 37% less overall surface area than four equivalent ranch-style houses of a similar volume. Less land is also used.

Such a townhouse could actually be made even more energy efficient if it was square in shape and had a flat, non-sloping roof. Square shapes need less external wall length for the same amount of internal volume than a rectangle. Thus, a square townhouse building would have 7.8% less surface area than Mom's rectangular unit. Although a square, three-level townhouse of the same volume would only decrease surface area by another 0.8%, it would dramatically lower overall land use by <u>33</u>%!

Although structurally more efficient, the individual units of a townhouse building are really no different than many separate, individual homes with many inefficient and duplicated living areas. Even conservatively speaking, the features of our individual homes are astronomically wasteful. On average, a home's six main activity areas sit unused a staggering <u>**92**</u>% of each and every day:

- Kitchens sit idle 95% of the time (for the purpose they are intended)
- Dining rooms sit idle 97% of the time (for the purpose they are intended)
- Living rooms sit idle 70% of the time
- Two bathrooms sit idle 94% of the time
- Game and exercise rooms sit idle 99% of the time
- Laundry rooms sit idle 98% of the time

Figure 11 – A sprawling townhouse community built entirely over wetlands.

These numbers are greatly compounded when homes don't just have one general living area or one dining room, but additional formal areas that are almost never used. My grandparent's home, for example, has both an eat-in kitchen and a formal dining room, which isn't even used on holidays anymore. They have a general living room, a second formal living room (used only to open presents and take naps in after large holiday meals), and actually even a third living area and bar in their completed basement. Like many homes, they also have a large front porch and back patio, which further compounds the problem. All of this mostly undivided internal and external living area is used by just three people.

Even the activity areas of our homes that are used during the day are seldom used to anything near their full capacity. For example, although most living rooms, dining rooms, and game rooms can comfortably accommodate five or six people, seldom more than half this number will ever be found using them at any one time—perhaps as few as just one person. A home's bathrooms provide another example. Because they are almost always undivided (without a separate shower room or separate toilet stalls) only one of its three functions (its toilet, sink, or its shower) can ever be used at any one time. This is why additional half-baths are necessary for those conflicting times.

Then there is always the lower-than-expected number of residents in each home to consider, which ends up wasting available bedroom space. Typically, homes are built for a family of four. However, out of the 30 homes I know of and have lived near, the average number of occupants per home was just 1.96. Thus, in the average half-empty house with just two occupants, 33% to 67% of the home's bedroom capacity goes completely to waste. Out of the 11 bedrooms in the four units of Mom's townhouse building, for example, only four bedrooms are used. Three of these four units have just one person living in them!

These revealing figures are <u>unreal</u> and costly to us all. These are not storybook times that we all seem to be designing our homes for. Yes, all of these various areas of a home— its kitchen, dining room, bathrooms, living room, and so on—*are* necessary. However, in a single-family home, they are used so infrequently that, for all intents and purposes, several other families could share these areas with us and we'd hardly ever even run into them. Thus, although structurally these larger townhouses gained some efficiency and cost-effectiveness through their economics of scale, they do not realize anywhere near their full potential because they fail to eliminate such internal duplications. Communal homes are naturally more efficient than this because they combine not just like features, but identical ones in proportions more equal to how much they are actually used.

More Complete and Fully Featured Living Areas

Within a carefully configured and streamlined communal environment, larger facilities can establish a level of completeness and quality far beyond that of individual homes. A shared communal kitchen, for example, can be made much more complete and fully featured than many smaller kitchens that use an identical set of inefficiently sized appliances. A shared communal kitchen would also cost less and take up far less space.

The equivalent volume of, say, six living rooms within six individual homes could be used much more diversely in a communal home. This same volume could be used for a home library, a pool table game room, an exercise room, a plush 16-seat home movie theater, an office with a fire safe and a server computer system, and even a craft room for things like sewing and pottery. Such diverse and high-quality living areas would benefit everyone in the home, and yet they do not take up any more volume than six ordinary/humdrum living rooms would.

Similarly, by using a single common kitchen, utility room, and dining area, we would not only keep these areas in use more often but also save enormous amounts of internal area that could then be used for still other, even more diverse purposes. With 70% to 85% less internal area devoted to kitchen, dining, and utility rooms (easily possible through proper planning), we would have the vital extra volume we need for:

- Large cabinetry and metal working shops for hobbyists and tradespeople
- Offices for private practices and home-based businesses
- Reception and customer waiting areas
- Supply and equipment rooms
- A conference and home schooling classroom
- Open martial arts training areas
- Larger segmented bathrooms that allow the individual toilet, sink, and shower areas to be used simultaneously without any loss of privacy

All of these additional features help add up to a far more defined, well-rounded, and more complete living environment that is free of wasteful duplication. They also help to demonstrate the communal home's most advantageous ability—the potential establishment of substantial, commercial-quality businesses right at the home level!

Having the potential for even simple home-based businesses like a barbershop could allow at least a few residents to earn a living at home without having to travel. The home already provides for our needs 75% of the year and is tasked with securing our belongings at all times. Thus, if we could expand the home's performance just this extra little 25% so that it allows at least some of us to work from home, we could eliminate the average hourly commute spent traveling to and from work. This would increase our free time by 10%! As we will see in Appendix F, not having to commute will also save us from having to own so many cars, and thus we can avoid the many costly travel-related expenditures that go along with them. Working at home is one of the *primary benefits* of a communal facility, which can afford and direct more internal volume to shops and offices than private homes do.

Organizing the Chores

In communal homes, the consolidation of many duplicated activities also becomes possible. All of the seemingly endless individual chores that each family would have had to perform on a one-by-one, family-by-family basis could become the support tasks carried out by three out of every ten residents as their contribution. Tasks such as:

Cooking meals	Shoveling snow/raking leaves
Washing dishes and doing housework	Dropping people off at work
Shopping for groceries	Taking the kids to:
Stocking shelves	After-school lessons/practice

Comparing prices and cutting coupons	The doctors
Looking after the pets	Taking the car in for inspection
Paying the bills and sorting the mail	Taking pets to the veterinarian
Taking care of the lawn and garden	Taking electronics in for repair

can all be coordinated and completed more efficiently by a small group of residents, than by each person trying to do these things on his or her own. Imagine being one of the residents who never has to cook, clean, or wash dishes again, and having six more hours of free time during the week to play with: an increase in free time of another 10%!

Similarly, the people doing these tasks on behalf of everyone else would enjoy additional free time as well. This is because all of their own chores are done as part of their contribution to the home. Thus they, too, would have their weekends entirely free of having to shop, mow the lawn, and clean: a win-win situation leading to a higher quality of living for everyone involved! Free time will really be free time, not just the only time you have left to get caught up on all the things you've pushed off to the weekend. This ratio of having one out of every three adults staying at home in support roles is also more proportional to the amount of housework that needs to be done. A one out of every two ratio, where one spouse stays home and the other works, is just too high to be cost effective.

Having such dedicated at-home workers to handle these tasks can be one of the most important arrangements that residents of a communal home can make. These chores can obviously be broken out or performed in turns, as one might normally think to do; however, trying to get everyone to partake in such an arrangement would probably end up as a source of tension between residents. It isn't hard to imagine how a complex agreement, as to who should do what as part of their share and when, would start to fall apart when people fell behind on tasks they only felt so so about. Tasking three or four of the home's residents with the equivalent of a part-time job performing such support functions is a more dependable way to eliminate this likely point of contention.

These are all tasks that people do at home and that others make a living at. As long as the people doing them are properly compensated (with, say, four weeks of vacation a year and a 32-hour workweek), I see no reason to view such work as demeaning or any less important than any other job. In fact, I think I'd find it desirable (having worked extensively at such jobs in the past) because I'd have more time to work on my own projects and greater job security than I have now. Having one additional day off a week (another 10% increase in free time) is certainly an increase in our quality of living!

Privacy Concerns

All of the efficiencies and benefits brought forth through the fundamental design aspect of economy of scale hinge, of course, on the use of a shared environment: a potential stumbling block for those accustomed only to life in a single-family home. We must realize, though, that single-family homes are just an ideal of society and not a design limitation. They are the embodiment of a "make it on your own" mentality and are built around a domestic relationship with a spouse and young children. The problem with this is that it is just an ideal. The realities of life are such that even under ideal conditions it has become very hard for working parents or single-parent families to keep up with the demands of life, let alone afford a home with a library and game room or save enough money for retirement. Our free time is consumed by chores that we don't have all that much time for after a full day's work. As a result, we often fail to eat right or get enough sleep or exercise, and attending such things as a college course is almost entirely out of the question, even if we could afford it.

During the free time that we do have, most people are likely to be found only watching television or a movie apart from sleeping in their respective private homes. If we must somehow insist that we can watch TV only with loved ones, we let slip the home's potential to secure a more comfortable and secure family life via the economy of scale of a larger, more fully featured communal home. Functional, high-performance bedrooms with PC workstations and their own entertainment centers could easily handle our personal TV viewing preferences, so why be so emphatic about that?

I don't think people realize that they actually spend 28% of their time with people they don't really know anyway—the people they work with. People certainly don't expect to know anyone at a restaurant, yet dining out is considered to be an enjoyable experience. I also find the use of large living room bay windows (which people typically don't much bother blocking off at night) and the occasional use of open-air bedrooms (such as lofts that have absolutely no privacy) also a bit ambiguous. They both seem to indicate (at least to me) a lack of concern for privacy. So why, with these sorts of conflicting things in mind, should we be so emphatic about living in an expensive private home where we must fight endlessly by ourselves to keep up with all the demands of life? Proper design techniques can be employed to make adjustments for this essential need, while at the same time incorporating so much more that we'd also want in a home, too!

The aspect of privacy is too finite and intangible to be given such top, overriding dominance in the design of something as critically important as a home. Besides, increasing the free time for every resident by 20%, as we have talked about, is like having *eight and a half years* of additional free time over a typical 45-year working career! Is that really worth giving up for a desire to watch TV and walk around your own home in your underwear? The amount of intimate time we spend with a loved one is dwindling at alarming rates regardless of whether we live in separate, private homes or not. Having more free time and being able to work at home in support roles or as the operator of a home business would actually start to bring this lost time back into our lives. To me, this additional **FREE TIME** is what it is all about!

Past Failures

Without such careful and deliberate reasons for living together that a true multifamily home provides, it is easy to see how the communes of the early '70s quickly fell out of favor. These were social experiments conducted by religious fanatics, freeloaders, and hormonally challenged youths, all of whom were experiencing an emotional roller coaster of social and political issues. Such experiments do not even come close to a fair test of multifamily living. Although we'd all like to forget those times, we need to ask ourselves whether these same experiments would have had a totally different outcome if they had been carried out by, say, a group of professionals and tradespeople (working at the edge of their respective fields) in homes specifically designed for them and their talents.

Enhanced Social Atmosphere

Provided the home design did not introduce its own points of conflict that would put residents in contention with one another (such as not having enough bathrooms or hot water), families and couples should have no trouble adapting to a level of privacy actually better than what they grew up with. In fact, couples of the same generation are not only less likely to mind having to share the kitchen and a low-light dining area with one another, they would surely enjoy the home's enhanced social atmosphere.

Having someone of the same age and interests around to do things with—and the many diverse recreational areas of the home to do them in—would provide a person with a wider variety of activities they could pursue. A two-person, husband and wife relationship often stagnates when there is little to do other than to watch television together. Men tend to enjoy certain activities, like sports and shooting pool. Most women do not. Women enjoy sewing and crafts. Most men do not. Therefore, having other women and men around to do activities with on a regular basis becomes a blessing to an otherwise one-dimensional relationship. Couples with children could get together nightly for card games or head out for weekend excursions to national parks together. Young teens would have their own close-knit group in the home and their own places to hangout, which is *much* safer for them. Communal living is simply the most natural, efficient, and downright fun way to live when it is done <u>correctly</u>!

Building a home around friendships as well as around a family should actually prove to be more enjoyable for everyone. Humans are social animals by nature and there's just too much to gain. Couples do need to have a place to think, read, and relax quietly together, and this fact will not be overlooked in the communal home designs that I am proposing.

*"Communal living is simply the most natural,
efficient, and downright fun way to live when it is done correctly!"*

Chapter Three

Life Within a Multifamily Environment

Choosing to live with several or perhaps dozens of other families is different than allowing your children to remain at home or granting them the freedom to return back home if they need to. As parents, we have a responsibility to our children: to raise them, and we certainly want to see them do well. Most friends, on the other hand, are—how can we say—merely acquaintances. We know them, but we don't necessarily want to live with them. Some friends we share our experiences and time with, but at the end of the day, we all go home to our private lives, which for many of us is our only source of sanity in this world. For us to, therefore, imagine living not only with our friends but with their families as well is a very foreign idea, not one we often entertain.

But imagine for a moment, if you will, being able to live with people you deeply respect—say, a martial arts instructor or a college professor who is the co-president of an exciting outdoor club. Say an excellent musician or a good mechanic. Imagine what you could learn from a tailor who is eager to teach you a craft and who can give everyone a better than average fit. The list goes on, but the point is that in order to live with someone, there needs to be a level of respect for what they've accomplished, not just a level of friendship or camaraderie. When you deeply respect someone, you'll go out of your way to make the situation of living together work. You won't necessarily grow annoyed with someone for simply forgetting to put something back where they found it. Don't you just hate that?

Although we may indeed respect those we live with and design homes to eliminate other potential problems, there is always the issue of finances: who contributes what, who decides what to buy when it effects everyone, and ultimately, who owns what. There may be issues concerning children and pets. A horde of children may be hard for any adult to cope with and many people have allergies and therefore can't have pets. There may also be issues concerning individual tastes, comfort levels, and idiosyncrasies. These are all issues that need to be addressed long before people can fully commit themselves to the concept of multifamily living, as well as the enjoyment of its many benefits.

Making Your Contribution

It must be understood up front that not everyone will be able to contribute equally. Professionals with a good reputation, many years of experience, and an established client base will certainly earn more than people just starting out. Those professionals that contribute monetarily to the home, such as the carpenters, mechanics, attorneys, and beauticians, will be fully supported by the at-home workers as mentioned previously. They won't have to worry about the cooking or any of the other everyday chores.

If the home or one of the cars needed repairs or a resident needed legal advice, then certainly, these professionals would be expected to offer their expertise to those who needed it. After all, this is part of the benefit of living with a highly talented group of people. But, for the most part, these people would wake up to things like a bacon and egg breakfast and come home to fully prepared meals with homemade bread and fresh garden vegetables that they wouldn't have had time to prepare otherwise.

Shedding 60% to 85% of their vehicle needs, daycare costs, and about five hours of travel time per week, highly skilled residents could launch an absolute renaissance in the quality of living that middle-class citizens can achieve. The combined purchasing power, skill, and background of such professionals can create a home economy nearly independent of corporate downsizing. Standing shoulder-to-shoulder, no one will have to question the services or the quality of work they receive when it comes from the people they trust—the people they live with! Craftsmanship will improve, skills will be passed on, and more durable, commercial-quality homes could be built with just the savings realized on commuting-related travel expenses alone. Tailored clothing, customized internal decorating, handmade furniture, and one-on-one martial arts instruction are all reasons for people to become fully involved.

Such professionals have a unique part to play in bringing this efficient form of living to the forefront of modern day society. Their participation will attract other talented people who will in turn make this entire plan work: a *cascading effect* to be sure! With homes that use 75% to 95% less land than an equivalent number of single-family homes and far less electricity to heat and cool, we can all feel proud to be a part!

At the other extreme, residents who may have lost their jobs and cannot contribute monetarily would simply stay at home and do what they would normally do: offer their support to the income-generating efforts of the others. Just two work-at-home residents, working 32 hours a week at the equivalent of, say, $8.50 an hour, would provide a service valued at $28,300 a year. This figure translates into $848,600 over a 30-year period. Having someone always at home provides a higher level of security. It saves working folks from having to take a half-day off work just to let the repairperson in or to take the kids to the doctors. Alternatively, people with a certain talent may be able to contribute in their own way. If a person does not have a particular talent that allows them to contribute, they may be asked to go to school to acquire one: a talent that the group as a whole feels it needs or that is in high demand in the area. There may be a position open as a receptionist at the attorney's office. Occasionally, a person who is free may be asked to go to the jobsite where the home's carpenter is working at, or to help out in the shop sanding or staining some furniture. In all, it is a group effort, where everyone is valued and nothing short of teamwork is acceptable.

The Organization of Spending

While living in a multifamily home, everyone is expected to exhibit an exceptional degree of prudence, group decision-making, and conformity when they spend their own money. Every appliance, stereo system, and vehicle must be carefully selected, through analysis of the best available consumer information, for its functionality and overall performance. Industrial-grade, high-performance products that will last must be selected, not cheap junk that people often buy on impulse. These produces will be far better than what residents would have been able to afford on their own. Like moving into a fully furnished apartment that has the latest HD-TVs, personal computers, and appliances, you just won't need to worry about buying very much. You can, in turn, save your own money for your vacation, your kids' college, and, perhaps, your own home.

Issues Concerning Vehicles

Cars especially, are one thing that everyone needs to decide on as a group. Because of the set, limited size of the vehicle-parking bay, we have to be very deliberate about the size and functionality of the vehicles we buy. Both the length and the width of a vehicle are critical factors to be carefully considered. A garage bay that is 64 feet (19.5 m) deep, for example, would have been specifically designed to fit four Honda *Civic-size* passenger cars, which are 14.6 feet (4.45 m) in length. If these four cars were parked end-to-end in such a garage, there would only be 13 inches (34 cm) of clearance between them. Throw in the purchase of some car that is longer than what was specifically intended, and you could have eliminated the ability to put a fourth car into the garage: a dramatic 25% reduction!

If it was decided, instead, that minivans were needed, then that's fine, too. A 64-foot-deep vehicle bay is also an ideal size for three minivans parked end-to-end, and would have enough clearance between them to get your luggage in and out of the back. Similar vehicle size constraints also apply to a vehicle's width. Combinations of thin and wide and long and short vehicles must also be considered in order to get the best, most flexible overall parking bay dimensions.

To make the most of the limited space available in the garage, vehicles need to be carefully scrutinized for a level of functionality and performance that will facilitate the unique demands of a shared multifamily environment. ***No luxury or sports cars would be allowed!*** Highly functional and efficient vehicles like vans and economy cars are critical.

Multifunction Vans

The very best and most fully equipped minivans and full-size vans (which are rapidly progressing in their abilities and features) would be sought despite their luxury car-sized price tag, and for good reason. Vans offer a very high seating capacity, which is vital for weekend trips and carpooling. The rear seats can be removed to offer a very functional, high-capacity cargo area needed for transporting shop supplies and groceries. The features of full-time four-wheel-drive and advanced traction control systems can provide all-weather dependability—a highly warranted feature given that we have more people depending on far fewer vehicles. Stronger multi-valve engines with variable-valve timing also give minivans the fuel economy of a passenger car, as well as the towing capacity of a pickup.

Fully featured vans are also ideal for extensive business travel and commuting. A foldout table in the rear allows today's business people (with their laptops and cell phones) to keep up with events at their respective offices when they don't have to focus on driving. They could check their voice messages, return calls, respond to e-mail, keep an eye on the weather, or enjoy a movie. Extremely comfortable seating, multiple climate-control systems, and an advanced stereo system are also features proportional to the demands of a long trip and a high degree of usage. Buying vans with a stronger engine and a fully featured interior actually allows us to make the greatest possible use of the vehicle and our time in it. Some features (like video monitors in the rear cabin) may seem like unnecessary luxuries when compared to the austere features found in most vehicles, but these vans will not just be sitting in the garage all night or out in the parking lot of a place of employment all day. Residents who depend on them will use them round-the-clock. A benefit of high use is a high level of features, and is—to some extent—our reward for combining our resources so deliberately.

Versatile Economy Cars

Commuter vehicles at the other end of the spectrum, like the Toyota Echo or Honda Civic, are sized more closely to the needs of an individual commuter with a long drive ahead of them. Commuting alone _is_ necessary when people work too far away to effectively take public transportation and when other residents cannot easily drop them off. If measured just by a factor of time, it is also more efficient. When individual commuting is warranted, we want to be able to achieve this in the most efficient and safest way we can.

Economy cars eliminate the excessive weight and drag of a larger car body and are far more efficient and less wasteful than an SUV driven by just one person. They are less expensive, they get far better gas mileage, and we can fit more of them into our vehicle bays. They are also constructed to be very safe. In the long term, I am very optimistic that flying cars **(Figure 12),** and other advanced VTOL aircraft can provide an even more efficient and faster way of taxiing people out over long distances.

Sharing and Standardizing Vehicles

Apart from purchasing cars that allow us to make the most of the limited size of our vehicle bays and that are tailored to the well-defined role laid out for them, we must also learn to share vehicles. Sharing vehicles is vital because a 64-foot-deep parking bay restricts access to those vehicles parked all the way at the back. Whoever comes home first will be parked into the back of the garage for a week. Sharing vehicles simply allows a person who needs a car or van to take the one that is at the front of the garage.

RVs and boats also need be shared. Much like a summer cottage that a large communal home might own, RVs and boats could operate nearly year-round, affording every couple and family at least one week of use a year. Here again, such high usage by everyone would warrant investing in a much more capable, multifunctional unit. This type of shared arrangement would be extended to a handful of boats, canoes, and top-quality mountain bikes that could serve the needs of everyone, while saving greatly on space.

The shared, communal use of vehicles and the potential role of an at-home worker as a dedicated driver, to shuttle people off to work and back, is also important because it enables us to get by with 1/6th the number of vehicles that would otherwise be needed **(see Appendix B on page 115).** That's an <u>84</u>% reduction! Having fewer vehicles allows us to drastically lower the amount of land needed for parking, and the extreme expense of a commercial-quality parking bay **(see Appendix C on page 120).** Taking the time to be so deliberate and concise about what we buy and how we use things can have a very positive effect on our world and on the quality of home and vehicles that we can afford. Buying vehicles of the same make and model can also be important because it simplifies maintenance and allows us to keep them running longer as we strip parts from older cars.

Ownership

How residents actually agree to pay for common-use items like stereos, cars, and appliances and who would eventually own them should people want to leave, is a very important consideration. Ownership in large communities is often handled by incorporating the community, typically as a nonprofit organization. In such a situation, no one actually owns the building or vehicles other than the corporation. If the corporation has to be dissolved, ownership of individual assets would be broken out according to provisions written into the corporate bylaws. Obviously, there are legal issues here, and how we are able to run the community may depend greatly on the regulations governing the type of corporation the community files for, which does vary. Bylaws are also used to spell out such things as who or what group makes the decisions, how much authority they have, and how voting takes place. Incorporating obviously has tax advantages for our home-based businesses, which makes incorporating that much more likely.

Groups of any size can incorporate; even individual people can. This could become as much of a practical solution for residents of individual, multifamily homes as it has become for large communities. Such legal arrangements do add a level of complexity that would, obviously, not be needed for smaller, extended-family homes, where individual ownership of items can be easily retained.

Still other groups may decide to forgo such legal complications, at least initially, by making some simple arrangements between themselves. People who want to remain cautiously optimistic (wanting to keep their options of moving out open to them) might pay a reduced rent to those in a core group who pay the mortgage. This method places ownership securely in the hands of the most dedicated person or persons, which is what I think I would prefer myself.

Other arrangements, involving the purchase of new appliances and cars, may not need to be made for some time, as people are simply going to move in with their own things and take their stuff with them when they go. This makes having ample amounts of bulk storage space critical, as it allows residents to keep their own furnishings in storage until they decide if this is the right place for them. When couples do start to purchase items for the group as a whole, it will be easy for them to decide whether to split the costs out among many or to buy the item outright so that each item has a specific owner. As mentioned previously, such arrangements can lead to better products that everyone can enjoy.

Figure 12 – A four-passenger Skycar that gets 20 mpg (Photo courtesy of Paul Moller)

Issues Concerning Children

Life within a shared environment has several other factors that need to be considered. Some people have a hard time coping with children, for example. Children can get pretty noisy sometimes, and an entire group of them can be hard for anyone to deal with. To help residents cope, we need to have dedicated kids' rooms that have their own play and study areas. Classrooms would also be needed in my largest designs.

With many recreation areas in the home provided for different tastes, it is likely that kids will gravitate to certain areas of the home, while parents gravitated to their own areas. A game room may be the popular hangout for teens and their friends. Other living rooms may be specifically for parents only. Residents may also decide to use one set of bedrooms on one side of the home for adults, while the noisy kids' bedrooms were on the opposite side. A guard station, machine-gun nest, and a shark-filled moat would properly divide the two. Teens in the middle would serve as fodder for the attacking Ninja kids, buying enough escape-time for the parents to reach the rooftop and board the awaiting escape helicopters. Ha-ha! It's all about proper planning… really! In larger homes, parents with children can even have their own entire level to themselves. So can young adults and elderly folks.

I personally believe that children growing up in a communal environment would benefit from seeing greater interaction among adults of the same gender. Husbands and wives interact far differently than two friends do. Both, although seemingly natural to us, are complex social behaviors that child learn by observing. A more diverse group of people would also give children a wider range of ideas. I'd personally make sure every child knew basic astronomy. In general, children within such an environment would grow up with more friends, parental supervision, and education than they might otherwise have had.

Issues Concerning Pets

Having pets is probably the most difficult issue to handle in the design of a communal home. Pets are a wonderful source of love and need a home just like the rest of us. However, allergies and the dangers of having a big dog around small children must also be considered. Even if the dog is gentle, a child may step on a paw or grab a tail and thus get a nip or a scratch in return. Medical science may provide a cure for allergies in the years to come, but that is still a ways off. State-of-the-art ventilation and filtering systems can also be put in place, but they, too, can go only so far.

If pets cannot be allowed into the main living areas of the home for these reasons, then it is certainly possible (in larger homes) to have a humanely-sized and cozy kennel area within the home that is isolated from other areas **(Figure 31 – Page 87).** The kennel can have veterinarian offices, bathing and grooming areas, and a separate ventilation system. There would be an enclosed dog run outside for them as well. Birds might be given a cage in the climate-controlled attic greenhouse where they would be allowed to occasionally fly around. In general, though, we must realize that one person's pet tends to become everybody's pet in a communal environment. A small group of pets should be enough love and affection to go around for everyone!

Issues Involving Personal Preferences

Concerning the issue of personal preferences, such as temperature settings and musical tastes, there is much that can be done in the design of the home to help minimize their effects on others. The heat and AC will be controlled individually in each room. As mentioned with children, an obvious choice is for people with similar preferences and tastes to choose bedrooms that are closer together. One section might focus around a particular taste in music and so on. Longtime friends would obviously group together. Such homes will also have numerous living rooms where people of similar ages and tastes can congregate to enjoy their favorite activities. In smaller homes, the potential for having widely different tastes is not as great because the core group would most likely have similar interests to start with or be such good friends that it didn't matter.

Hopefully, the residents of such homes will represent an average slice of middle-class Americans just wanting to be more efficient and smarter about life. As such, I believe they will need to maintain an atmosphere of normalcy that everyone will find acceptable. Things like nudity, poor hygiene, and religious extremes would have to be highly prohibited to maintain this. I also believe there should be a "Don't ask—Don't wish to know" policy towards sexual preferences, where all romantic displays are kept private.

Handling Problems

The potential of having a member who is downright annoying is a problem that the design of the home can go only so far to address. Plenty of separate activity and work areas are be available for people to use, but that is about where such design solutions end. For those people who "can ruin the whole ambience of the situation" as one former college student (Tracy Skorka – Psych graduate of Penn State University) once said of dorm life, we must rely on sound human relations to handle such problems.

Conflict resolution was brought to a science after 30 years at the Twin Oaks community in Louisa, Virginia. People there advised being aware of your feelings and communicating them in a way that is not harmful. They recommended group meetings structured so that everyone could be heard and the use of a mediator to help resolve a problem between two people. They also had a very simple feedback culture to handle all of the not so serious matters.

People would communicate what they felt in a formulated way: stating the issue they had, the emotion they felt, the reason they felt like that, and the outcome they desired. They would first ask a person they needed to talk with if they were open for feedback. If the answer was yes, they would simply use the formula to state "when you (physical)... I feel (emotion)... because (reason). Instead, I would prefer (expectation)..." where the conversation was kept positive. An important part of this formula was to have concrete specifics such as "Dave, three times this week we had dried oatmeal stuck to the sink." They also said, from experience, that it is a mistake to think you know the right solution to the problem, so always be open to what the person you are confronting thinks in return.

In more serious situations—say if a member was threatening people—there are organizational ways of dealing with such matters. The community's bylaws may call for a vote to be taken in which only 25% of the vote is required to evict someone like this. This is because having as few as just 25% of the home's residents unhappy or outraged with the situation will affect everyone, and this is not what we are here for.

Foremost in avoiding such difficulties are proper methods of prevention. Screening and voting on new comers could be made a very deliberate and well-thought-out process. Want-to-be members may have to visit for an extended period so that they get to see if they will be happy there and if current members will accept them. Specific screening tests to find any tendencies toward racism, ageism, or sexism can be used, background checks and face-to-face interviews can be conducted, and voting to admit a new member may require an 85% majority before someone is accepted in.

Chapter Summary

Surely, life in a closely spaced, shared environment will be a test of character. Admitting when you're wrong or guilty, suppressing any jealousy and anger, and being open to other opinions can be hard to do at times. There may be times when people don't feel like talking to you or exchanging a salutation. Some people only prefer direct, meaningful conversation or none at all.

Coping with a fellow resident's quirks and organizing finances, hopefully among people you respect, can be difficult. These issues force us to seriously consider whom we choose to live with and makes finding a group that is right for us that much more important. We are, however, social animals that indeed thrive in such an environment, as opposed to the isolation of a small, isolated nuclear family unit with the TV as our only companion.

I do think that people would argue less with their spouses, and things like child abuse, which would be impossible to hide, would vanish as well. I also like to think that having substantial home-based businesses can have a tremendous fusing effect, drawing residents closer together around a common goal!

Chapter Four

Advantages of Home Businesses

Working at home is the most direct and effective method of applying your personal productivity.[7] Those of you who have never had a chance to work from home may not appreciate just how much more productive you tend to be, as opposed to working for an outside employer. It is not uncommon to put in 12, 16, or even 18 hours a day into a project, while being so engrossed in it that you overlook eating. "You just don't notice it," Terry Brown—a three-year computer programmer—indicated in reference to working 80 to 90 hours a week at home. He works side-by-side with his wife, Linda—a 17-year programmer—and they both could not express how great it was for them and their children. They even went as far as saying that working 80 to 90 hours a week at home was "still better" than working 40 to 50 hours a week at an office.[8] Self-reliant people are also much more productive when they work at home. According to the college textbook *Management and Organization:*

> *"Productivity is likely to increase when work is moved into the employee's home. Where direct measurements have been possible, they have indicated that productivity increases on average about __50%__ in such situations. For example, a market research firm in New York moved certain work projects into the home in order to tap a wider labor market and save on office space. Data-entry productivity increased 30 percent over when the projects were conducted in the office."*

The book went on to estimate that in 1991 "26.6 million Americans (a full ten percent of the workforce) conducted their work from their own home (ten million of them operating their own businesses)." Free from the demands of travel or the need for daycare services, residents could establish their own:

---

[7] Management and Organization
[8] Terry and Linda Brown – October 29th, 1998

BUSINESSES BASED ON IN-HOME SHOPS AND SERVICES

Law Practice	Gunsmith	Chiropractor
Insurance Agent	Arts and Craft Shop	Alternative Medicine
Realtor	Carpentry/Cabinetry	Veterinarian
Tax Preparation	Furniture Refinishing	Print Shop
Financial Service	Reupholstering	Photo Studio
Architectural Office	Custom-Made Draperies	Beauty Salon
Martial Arts Studio	Shoe Repair	Florist
Music Studio/Instruction	Leather Goods	Small General Store
Appliance Repair	Tailor	Coffee Shop
Auto Repair/Restoration	Dentistry	Pizza Parlor
Jeweler/Goldsmith	Optometrist	Fresh Produce/Bakery

BUSINESSES BASED ON WORK AND UTILITY VEHICLES

Electrician	Welding	Septic System Cleaning
Plumber	Vehicle Towing	Commuting/Taxi Service
Home Remodeling	Caterers	Ambulance Service
Landscaping/Excavating	Chimney Cleaning/Repair	Snow Removal

Such businesses require features that are most often absent from contemporary homes. Almost never do we see a home with customer parking areas **(see Appendix D on page 122),** storefronts, dedicated offices, handicap accessibility, or a vital extra parking spot in the garage for a large work truck **(Figure 13).** A typical home's basement is also inadequate for most business-related activities. Basements tend to have very low ceilings and abound with clutter (due to a lack of closet space upstairs). They are often required for features that belong upstairs—such as a playroom and a casual living room—but that have been pushed downstairs to make room for extravagant formal areas. Basements occasionally contain the home's garage and furnace, which (on top of everything else) doesn't leave much room for anything but the smallest workshop.

Providing the Necessary Work Areas in a Home

By means of more residents to afford larger and more complete facilities, a true high-performance multifamily home can incorporate and staff a diversity of trade and professional businesses that are just not possible from the confines of contemporary homes. Many two- and three-level homes along the main street of a small town do have small street-level storefronts **(Figure 14)** and are quite successful. But multifamily homes (like the 11-, 12-, and 23-bedroom homes that follow; see **Figures 15 through 27)** would expand upon this tremendously! With as many as **15** workshop and office areas, residents could operate as many as six service-oriented businesses. There will be a customer reception desk, customer parking and waiting areas, offices, shops, and the home's garage will be large enough for even an ambulance-sized work truck and its respective supplies.

Figure 13 – An 8-foot-wide utility truck   *Figure 14 – Mama's Pizza (Derry Street)*

These homes also give residents the room they need to work on their hobbies. Supporting both hobbies and businesses is fundamental to a true multifamily home, which capitalizes on the broader skills of its residents. Personal projects or interests such as sewing and hunting (which are of a self-sufficient nature) help residents meet most of their own basic needs. The restoration of an old car, the making of a complicated dress, and the drawing of a floor plan are all activities that require a place where a person can get deeply involved in a project. A good number of these hobbies involve a lot of tools and materials that are actually more organized in what would appear to be a disorganized state than they are after they've all been put away. I like to call this work in progress. When you're busy and have things all spread out, normally over the dining room table, you don't want to have to stop and put everything away when it's time to eat. With large project-oriented rooms, however, you can just leave your things the way they are so you can jump right back into your project without delay.

When a person becomes good enough at a hobby to warrant good income, a dedicated project room and advanced shops **(see Appendix E on page 124)** are absolute must haves! Having a place to keep things organized is nice when you have an involved project of your own, but it's absolutely critical when you are trying to earn a living at it. The 25 to 30 minutes a day that it takes to put all your things away or to pull them back out again could mean the difference of whether you earn a profit on a project. When more people are involved, such as in a multifamily home, it is also not possible to leave your stuff lying all around in the dining or living areas, where there would be many more distractions to you as well. The important thing to remember is that to do more in a home, we need more room and more specialized work areas and tools, which in turn requires the added financial support of more residents.

The Elimination of Travel-Related Expenses

Not only does an in-home business afford residents more time with their families, it eliminates things like daycare costs (which average about $7,200 a year) and the frustration of traffic. The vital extra capacity that it would take to permit a fully functional business to be established in the home is also well worth its added cost when we consider what even a small multifamily home could save in travel-related expenses. The costs directly related to the time you would otherwise spend traveling to work, as well as automotive expenses, are listed in Appendix F on page 126. The more remote the place of residence, the worse the weather tends to get, or the greater the traffic is in an area, the greater these expenses would be.

Better Homemade Products and Self-Sufficiency

By working at home and making things for ourselves we benefit from the extremely high-quality items that can be made. As a person who sews, I can tell you that the clothes that you can make for yourself are virtually indestructible compared to those you can buy at a store. I, for example, emplace six rows of straight stitches and one row of zigzag stitching on every seam. This is in contrast to the two straight-stitch lines and one row of zigzag stitches usually found on store-bought products. By turning down my stitch length, I also emplace three stitches for every one stitch found on mass-produced clothing. Handmade clothes can also fit better and can be made with any specialized feature you can think of.

Overcoming our dependency on a constant need for outside interaction with society to sustain our every need is also something that we, as an advanced civilization, really need to address. Before we can bring forth an age where the implementation of high technology can take place without inconveniencing those that it puts out of work, we must have first stabilized ourselves, in advance, for such transitional times. Being able to provide for our own needs so that we can pick up after losing a job as if nothing has happened is something of a science, but it is possible. We would basically ride the push of our advancing technology as it surged forth to give us the time we need, as a culture, to expand our sciences and arts. We would contribute our time and talent, when they were needed, but not just to support a cyclic process that was out of control.

It isn't really that hard to envision how we might be able to stabilize ourselves to such a degree. One day, when homes are more efficient and solar panels are stronger, the gap between the power required by the home and that being produced may be nonexistent. This energy might even allow us to extract enough hydrogen from water to power our own fuel cell-powered vehicles. Once the home is paid for, we would be, essentially, free to live!

Outside Employment

Outside employment is by no means ruled out. In fact, providing a sure method of commuting back and forth to an outside job can be seen as a backup for residents to generate income if their in-home business should fail or be seasonally related. Bad location, too much competition in a given field, poor quality of the services performed, or the potential that someone who lived in the home did something that caused customers to shy away from our services are all things that would warrant having such a backup.

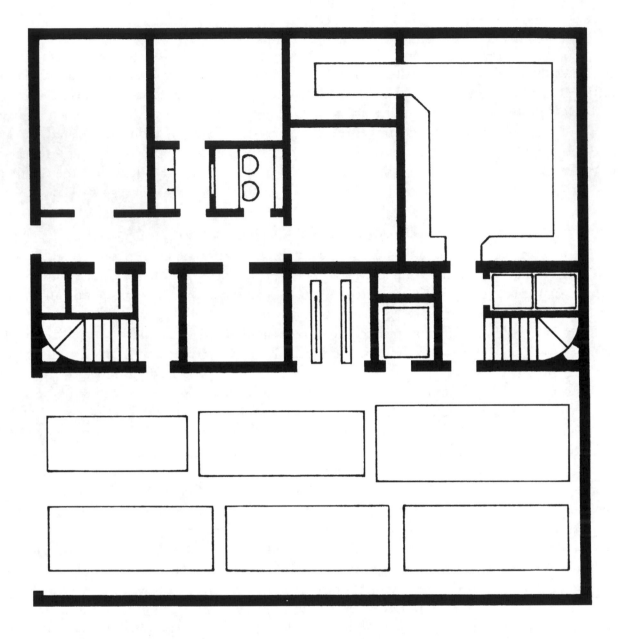

Figure 15 – Level 1 (Partial Basement):

This four-level, 11-bedroom, 57.6 x 59.4 home has 13,685 square feet overall and uses 75% less land than an equivalent number of single-family homes. It would cost 1.5 million dollars.

Upper right is a large 18 x 23 woodshop and a separate 8.5 x 11.2 workbench room. Center right is a stairwell with a storage closet under a portion of it. The garage (bottom) is shown with four minivan/SUVs, one Honda Civic-size vehicle, and one ambulance-size work truck. Bumper-to-bumper separation is 14 inches and side-to-side separation is a minimum of 30 inches. A small side bay adjoining the garage (center) can hold two motorcycles or an ATV. The home's elevator and vent shaft is to the right of this motorcycle parking area. Upper left are four easy-to-access business offices varying in size from 9 x 10 to 11.3 x 17.7. A three-bench-seat waiting area, a two-station reception desk, and a small half bath under the left-hand stairwell support these offices. Residents can access the elevator and stairs without having to enter into customer-oriented areas. Stairwells are 53 inches wide and the hallways throughout the home are a full 59 inches wide.

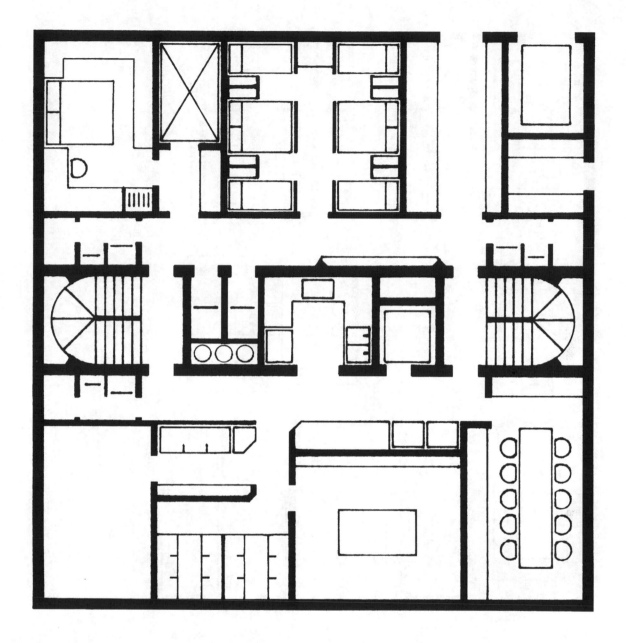

Figure 16 – Level 2 (Living):

Upper left is one of the home's eleven 11.2 x 17.7 master bedroom suites. Top center is a sixteen-person bunk bed visitors' room. Upper right are two ground-level lawn and garden closets, and an 18-foot-long breezeway rear exit. This back exit is lined with bicycle and gear racks and is wide enough to maintain or make ready two bicycles for the trail. At both ends of the upper hallway are two half bathrooms. In the center of the drawing are two separate shower rooms with their own hot water heaters and a 9.2 x 11.3 kitchen. Below the kitchen—along the corridor—is a serving counter and a pantry area with two additional refrigerator/freezer units. Below the left-hand stairwell are a third half bath and an 11.2 x 17.7 living room. To the right of the living room is a small open-air library/reading area as well as a two-booth, 12-seat dining room. The dining room has a stereo and television for evening get-togethers. Bottom center is a 14.8 x 17.5 pool table game room with enough library shelving for as many as 1,500 volumes. Lower right is a ten-seat 12 x 23 craft and home schooling conference room containing ample storage shelving and office abilities.

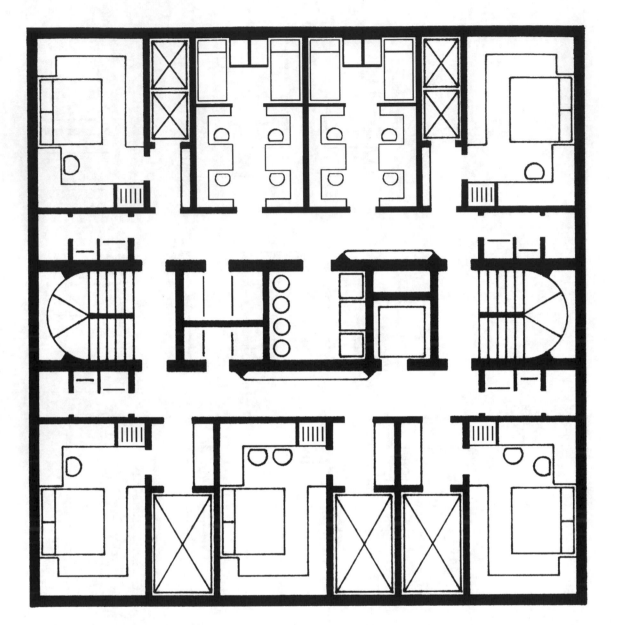

Figure 17 – Level 3 (Sleeping):

Top center are two children's bunk bedrooms for up to three children each. These rooms also have play and study areas. Running across the bottom and in the upper two corners are five additional master bedrooms for couples and singles to use. Each bedroom is shown with a king-size bed and a 12-foot-long desk area for PC workstations and an entertainment center. They also contain 25 feet of cabinet, drawer, and clothing storage racks. The doorway to each bedroom is placed away from the corners of the room to help maximize the amount of internal wall length available to place furniture against. Four half baths can be found at the ends of each hallway. In the center are two separate shower rooms and the home's laundry room (with four hot water heaters). The laundry room is on the main sleeping level where most of the laundry comes from. The walking distance from the bedrooms to either a bathroom or one of the stairwells is negligible. There is an average of **53 square feet** of bulk storage available per bedroom.

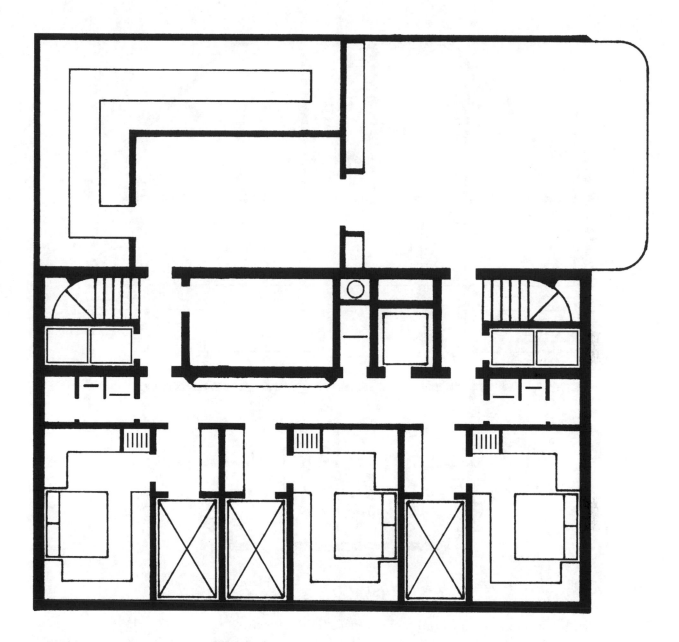

Figure 18 – Level 4 (Rooftop):

This upper level would appear to be only three floors aboveground when viewed from the back and from the sides. Across the bottom are three additional master bedroom suites and two half baths. These bedrooms (like those below) have a unique off the hall double-door side entryway that increases privacy, provides access to a **70-square-foot** bulk storage closet, and which helps to separate the bedrooms. This side entryway also provides seven of these bedrooms with a vanity sink, allowing couples to consolidate all of their personal hygiene items. In the center of the drawing are a shower room and a 9.2 x 15 exercise/weight room. Just above the weight room is a large 13.6 x 21.3 living/recreation room. Upper right is the home's massive 23.6 x 31 patio sundeck. Such a rooftop deck is great for entertaining, is more private (because it is up so high), and is appropriately sized as a landing area for future Vertical TakeOff and Landing (VTOL) Skycars. In the upper left corner is a hydroponics/greenhouse that provides a respectable **52 square feet** of growing area per resident. On this level, additional storage space is available above the stairwells.

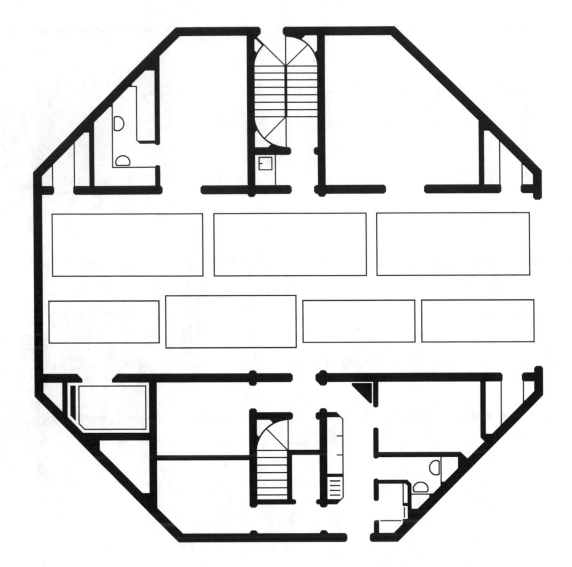

Figure 19 – Level 1 (Partial Basement):

This four-level, 12-bedroom, 66.5-foot-wide home has 15,016 square feet overall and uses 75% less land than single-family homes. It's called *"360"* and would cost $1.65 million.

Running across the center is a 23.3 x 65 garage bay shown with three 8 x 20 work trucks, a minivan, and three Honda Civic-size vehicles. At 14 feet high, the bay can hold semis, RVs, and farming and construction equipment. It also has elevating rafter platforms so that if the vehicles below are not very tall, the rafters can store small boats, ATVs, mountain bikes, and even other cars.

Surrounding the bottom stairwell are three offices (ranging from 9.5 x 12 to 9.2 x 13.3), a three-seat waiting area, a two-seat reception office, and a half bath by the bottom entrance. Since these offices are only 7.5 feet high, there can be a substantial 5.9-foot-high storage area above them for law and garden equipment. Bottom left is an 8.5-foot-deep fright elevator and two vent shafts.

Left of the upper stairwell is an 11.3 x 19.7 shop and a side workbench room that keeps the workbench area separate from the fumes, sparks, and dust generated in the shop. The stairwell is 47 inches wide (on both sides) and has bulk storage space underneath. Right of the upper stairwell is a 19.7 x 20 general-purpose workroom. At three of the four corners of the garage bay are three small storage closets for work vehicle and automotive supplies, driveway support items, recyclables, an emergency generator, and an air compressor. A commercial trash dumpster is used outside.

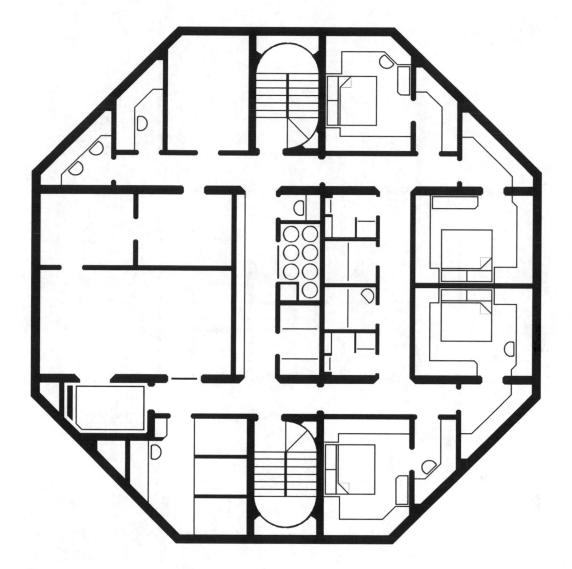

Figure 20 – Level 2:

On the right-hand side are four 11.3 x 15.1 bedrooms. Each bedroom has a side entryway, between 22.3 and 28 feet of closet storage length overall, and a 14-foot desk. The rectangular island of seven small rooms just right of center contains two half baths, two separate shower rooms, a full bath, a room with seven hot water heaters, and a phone booth (upper left). No bedroom borders a bathroom. The average walking distance from a bedroom to a half bath is 14.8 feet. The average walking distance from a bedroom to a stairwell is 26.7 feet.

Along the vertical corridor just left of center is a 23-foot-long floor-to-ceiling library shelf for collectable displays and up to 2,515 volumes. To the left of the bottom stairwell is a visitor's bunk bedroom with six full-size, bottom-entry bunks for six to 12 people. The visitor's room has storage shelving for suitcases and a small work desk for a PC.

Center left are three bulk storage rooms (ranging in size from 9.5 x 12.1 to 13.5 x 25) that provide an average of **47.2 feet of bulk storage space** per bedroom. If less storage is needed, the two smaller rooms can be used as den-size living rooms or project workrooms.

To the left of the upper stairwell, is a 10.5 x 15.1 living room. To the left of the living room are a small project room and a home office with corporate telephone and server computer systems, individual mailboxes, a Muzak sound system, and security and climate monitoring stations.

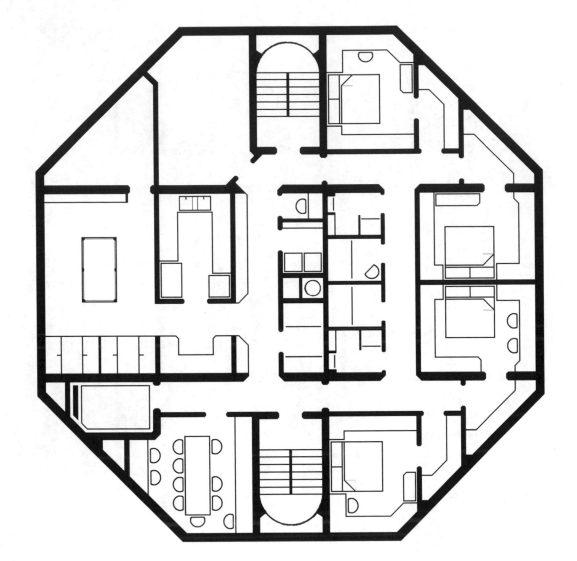

Figure 21 – Level 3:

Similar to the level below, there are four bedroom suites on the right-hand side. Bedrooms are deliberately stacked over each other so as to not be over nighttime living areas. The rectangular island just right of center is identical to the one below with the exception of having a laundry room and only one hot water heater, instead of seven water heaters. Such consolidated plumbing not only saves on initial construction cost and future maintenance, but it also lowers the amount of time you have to run the water for it to become warm. There is a 2.6-foot-wide plumbing shaft by the hot water heater, which is aligned with the one directly below.

Along the vertical central corridor is an array of 16-inch-deep pantry shelving and cabinet units that run floor-to-ceiling for 18 feet overall. The 13.6-foot-long kitchen just left of the hallway pantry is 9.3 feet wide and contains both a regular refrigerator and a 4.6-foot-wide commercial refrigeration unit. Just below the kitchen is a serving counter/kitchenette/beverage bar.

Center left is a 14.4 x 23.3 pool table game room with booth seating for eight. The triangular-shaped room at the upper left is an exercise room for up to five pieces of exercise equipment. The exercise room has an array of windows for a pleasurable atmosphere.

Left of the lower stairwell is an 11-seat conference/craft/classroom with ample storage space. Left of the upper stairwell is the home's main 12 x 19.7 living room.

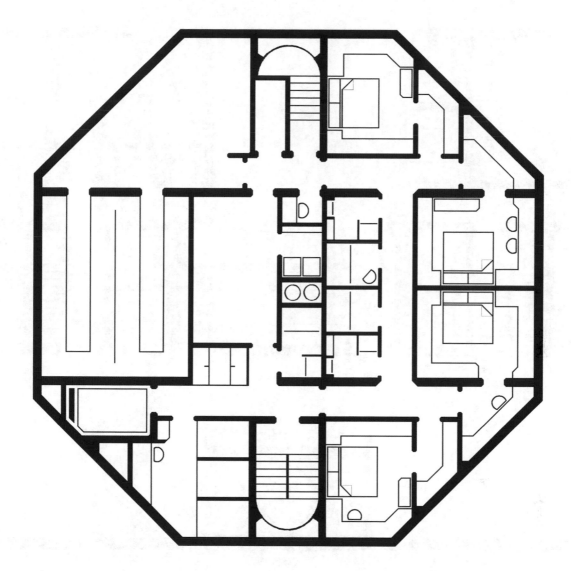

Figure 22 – Level 4:

On this level we see a similar combination bedroom and bathrooms with a second laundry room and two hot water heaters. Just left of the bathroom and laundry island is an 11 x 18.9 living room, which gives the home three living rooms in total.

To the left of the lower stairwell is a second visitors' bunk bedroom with storage and desk space. Just above the visitor's bedroom and just below the living room is a four-seat restaurant-like dining booth for basic activities and morning coffee.

Center left is a large rooftop greenhouse for year-round food production. The greenhouse has 3.3-foot-deep shelving units stacked four high to provide 1,300 square feet of growing area. That works out to **54.2 square feet** for every person in the home at maximum capacity. Artificial lighting is used on the lower shelving units.

Upper left is a large patio/terrace with a partial roof overhang. Such a semi-enclosed patio would be great for morning Tai Chi and yoga and there is plenty of space for an outdoor entertainment center and a generous amount of outdoor couches and coffee tables. A large closet to the right supports the patio area. It is located over part of the stairs coming up.

The rooftop above is open and flat with a central landing area for a medium-lift helicopter or several flying cars. Juniper gardens form an efficient living rooftop around the outside.

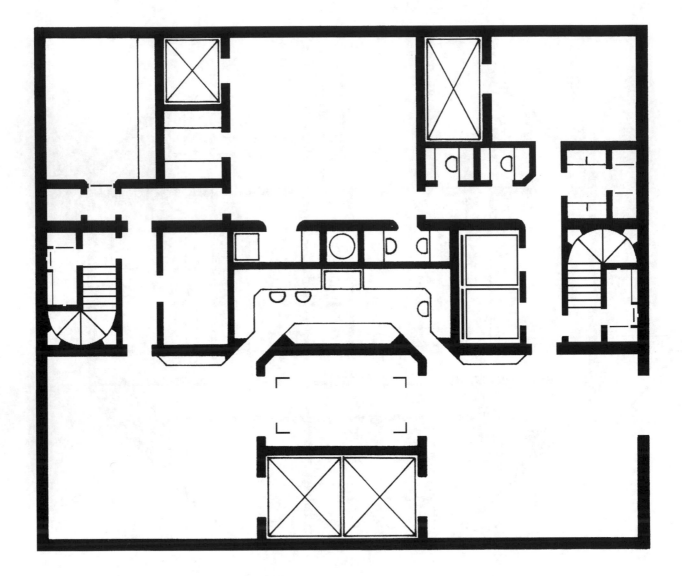

Figure 23 – Level 1 (Basement/Shop):

This next six-level, 23-bedroom, 67 x 78.7 home design (called *"Concurrence"*) has 31,608 square feet overall and uses <u>86%</u> less land than an equivalent number of 14.2 single-family homes (with an average of 2.6 residents) and six businesses. It costs about $3.4 million and is meant for a group of professionals working at the edge of their respective fields.

Top center is a 23.6 x 23.6 open martial arts center with and two conversion closets (left) for extra furniture, folding tables and chairs, and cots. These items allow the room to be converted to different functions as needed during non-training hours. There is also a small kitchenette and a two-person office just below the training center. Upper left is a large music room. Upper right is a 13.8 x 18.7 exercise/weight room, a closet for extra equipment, two small sit-down phone booth/changing rooms, a four-seat waiting room, and a small shower room.

Across the bottom are two large 23.6 x 27 wood and metal shops. A shop storage area and an engine-dismantlement bay are located between them. Center is a 28-foot-long workbench room that connects the two shops and is separated to prevent dust and sparks from entering in. Center left is the back stairwell and an 8.5 x 14.4 project room. Center right is the lead stairwell and two elevators. Two half baths are located below both stairwells on either side.

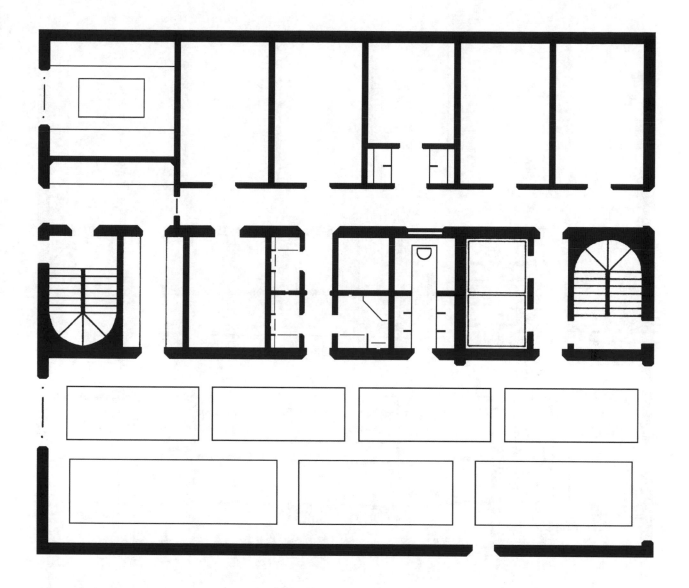

Figure 24 – Level 2 (Garage/Office):

The 11-foot-high parking garage (bottom) is shown with four minivan/SUVs, two ambulance-size work trucks, and even a 25-foot-long work truck (bottom left). Side-to-side vehicle separation is a minimum of 2.6 feet. Bumper-to-bumper separation is at least 20 inches. An alternate row of five Honda *Civics* is possible but there'd only be 8 inches of bumper-to-bumper separation. A unique driveway elevator, which lowers flush with the driveway and can be driven over, provides parking for two additional minivans and access to the lower-level shops and to various motorcycles, canoes and extra fuel stored under the driveway.

Upper left is an exterior lawn and garden closet that also stores 10 MTBs. The breezeway exit (below this) is lined with shelving for things like yard games, maintenance supplies, and bolt-on window shields that are used to protect the home during severe storms. Across the top are five offices (four are 11 x 18 in size) and a four-seat waiting area for a wide variety of home-based businesses. In the center are a reception desk, a six-seat waiting area for residents waiting for a ride, two half baths (one for customers), a full bath, a sixth 10 x 14.4 office, and a storage room (inward of the left-hand stairwell) for car care items, child safety seats, and work vehicle supplies. A square ventilation, plumbing and wiring shaft can also be seen in the exact center.

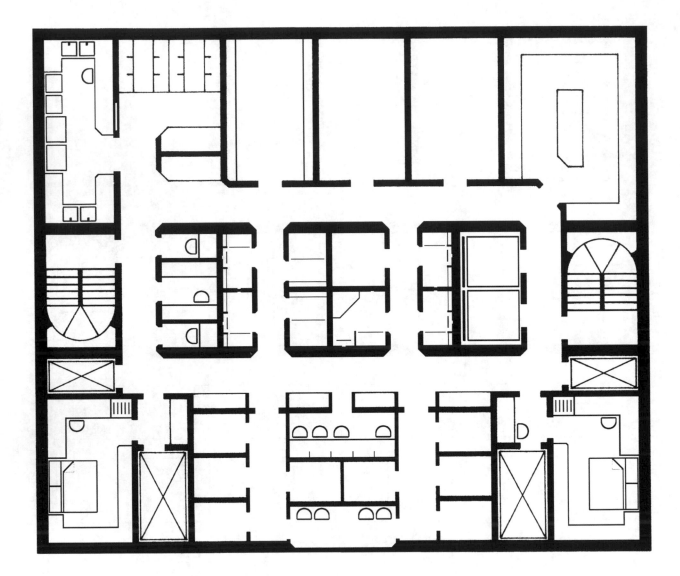

Figure 25 – Level 3 (Living):

Across the top there is the main 9.1 x 23.6 kitchen (upper left), a 12-person/two-booth dining area, three 11 x 18.3 living rooms, and a 17 x 23.6 craft/home-schooling/conference room. The kitchen has two 26-cubic-foot refrigerator/freezers, two stoves, four sinks (two extra large for scrubbing pots), 2.6-foot-deep pantry shelving, and 20 feet of countertop length. The dining room has two 7.9-foot-long serving counters with a beverage bar. Below the dining room are a phone booth, a small home office, and a second phone booth for visitors to use.

In the bottom corners are two of the home's 11.1 x 18.4 master bedrooms with their own bulk storage rooms and side entryways (which helps to separate them). Each master bedroom has a 14-foot-long office desk, 24 feet of wardrobe shelving and clothing racks, and allowances for a king-size bed. Bottom center are two 16-person bunk bed visitors' rooms with 16 queen-size bunk beds, storage shelving along the hall for suitcases, a five-station PC support room, and even a small 14.4-foot-long terrace where visitors and residents can take in some fresh air.

In the center of the drawing are four half baths (with urinals), a full bath, two separate shower rooms (with full bathtubs), and the ventilation shaft that will contain six oversized hot water heaters right next to where all three showers are.

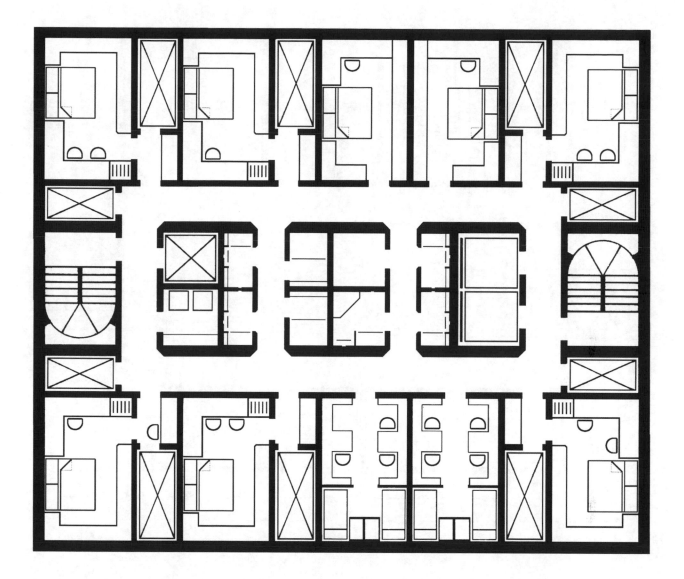

Figure 26 – Level 4 and 5 (Sleeping):

Across the top and bottom of this design are 10 additional master bedroom suites. Bedroom doorways are widely separated to increase privacy. They are a minimum of nine feet apart. Dividing walls are eight inches thick and eleven additional bulk storage rooms help to further separate things to lower noise levels. This level is located as far away as possible from the noise of the home's shops and music rooms found in the basement.

The average walking distance from the bedrooms to one of the stairwells is 27 feet. The average walking distance from the bedrooms to the closest bathroom is 17.7. These distances are easier to transit given the use of 55-inch-wide hallways, which allow two people to pass one another without having to pause.

The three showers on this level allow all potential occupants to shower within 1.6 hours. Because the bathrooms are segregated into separate shower and toilet areas, they can be used simultaneously without any loss of privacy. Six of the ten bedrooms on this level also have their own vanity sink areas for use during morning routines. Center left (inward of the hall and stairwell) is a laundry and utility room as well as a small bulk storage closet. Overall, the home has 6 showers, 6 bathtubs, 22 toilets, 18 urinals, 43 vanity sinks, and two laundry rooms.

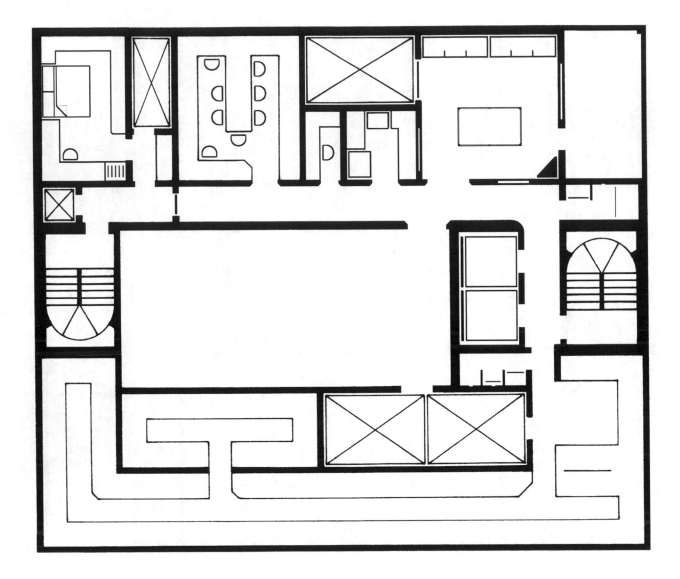

Figure 27 – Level 6 (Activity):

This level has a massive indoor 20 x 42 multiuse ***racquetball court*** (center). Such a facility has many potential uses. It can be used for gymnastic training, indoor basketball, for a variation of volleyball (known as walleyball), as a conference center, a pool table game room, a training center, or as an emergency bed-down area for disaster victims. The entire back wall of the court also folds down to reveal 46 spacious movie theater seats! In order to support such a variety of potential uses, there is a large 9.5 x 26 conversion closet directly below it (bottom center). Everything from extra furniture and game tables to folding chairs and cots can be stored for quick and effective use.

Facing south, the bottom half of this drawing houses a massive U-shaped hydroponics greenhouse/arboretum that provides each of the home's 46 residents with **76 square feet** of vegetable-growing area (on racks three feet deep stacked four high).

Across the top are another master bedroom, a large craft room, a phone booth/storage closet, a second kitchen with bar, a conversion closet with extra games and furniture, a game room/living area, and a patio deck (upper right). In all, the home's 23 bedrooms have an average of **64.5 square feet** of bulk storage capacity each. Two bathrooms can also be seen (center right). The rooftop above this level has an open patio and landing area for future flying cars.

Cost-Effectiveness

At $110.00 per square foot, this 23-bedroom facility would cost 3.4 million. Although an equivalent number of 14.2 separate homes (with 2.6 people each) would technically only cost around 2.8 million, they would use seven times more land and would not boast the features, office/work areas, or the commercial-quality construction that this home has.[9] Estimated savings in travel-related expenses for 20 of the home's residents who can work at home is $950,000 over a typical 30-year mortgage period. $210,000 could be saved on daycare costs when caring for just a single child on average over this same timeframe. $1.5 million could be saved on nursing home expenses while caring for just one elderly resident on average, too. The economy of scale of combining so many homes into one and using a more efficient shape, also allows this facility to have about 70% less roof area and 50% less external surface area exposed to the elements. Such an overall reduction makes the home much more efficient to heat and cool and far less expensive to maintain.

Residents would also save more in such a home by carpooling. Children's things would be passed on and things like top-of-the-line boats and RVs would be shared. Residents would save when purchasing fewer, longer-lasting appliances, electronics, and garden and shop tools. Health club and martial arts class dues as well as automotive labor bills would also be saved. The cost of land would be lower, and residents could more easily absorb the cost of solar panels, fuel cells, and co-generators, which single families can't hope to afford on their own. It can also be argued that contemporary homes are not built very durably and last only half as long as they could. Thus, their long-term maintenance and replacement costs would be much higher.

Work Support and Other Sources of Income and Savings

At 80% capacity, there would be as many as 30 working age adults in this home. With **15** offices, shops, and workrooms in the home, all residents should be able to work right from home as either small business proprietors or in supporting roles. To support this, there would be an 80-line phone system, an interlinked server computer system, and parking capacity three large work trucks. The home's six ground-level offices can alternate from serving up to three patient/client-oriented businesses (such as a law practices, hair salon, or a dental office) to serving as small storefronts for things like a furniture store. Depending on customer demand, several offices can also be combined into a massive 23 x 33 open section for something like a small restaurant or large retail store.

Apart from the home's normal work areas, there is also a great potential to use the eight-person martial arts training in the basement to earn as much as $320 a day or almost $80,000 a year in class dues from outside practitioners! Since the home's racquetball court can also be converted into a 46-seat home movie theater or conference center, there is a potential here too to earn as much as $18,000 during a one-week conference. Live performances and plays can also be given in this exceptionally useful center/court.

The rooftop hydroponics garden is also a substantial money saver. These year-round gardens can produce ten times **(10X)** the volume of fresh vegetables compared to an equivalent plot of farmland (saving land) and provide 110% of the fresh vegetable needs of the home's residents. Growing vegetables this way uses less water, fewer—if any—pesticides, and it prevents soil erosion. There would also be a deck/juniper garden directly over the customer parking areas.

---

[9] I use 2.5/2.6 as an average of comparison because individual homes do not have the ability to support adult couples in every available bedroom and usually have only two occupants each from my experiences. They also don't have enough storage or privacy and wouldn't have any room left available for visitors if all bedrooms were occupied. 2.6 is also the national average per household.

Environmental and Personal Benefits of Working at Home

Ecologically, the single-family home's casual nature and overwhelming lack of performance has played a decisive role in the unchecked destruction of our ecology. The sprawl of our local shopping malls and all the other one-level businesses that line our built-up thoroughfares is largely created through the lack of self-sufficiency in the home. If you think about it, **almost anything a service economy can do, we can do better in the large shop and work areas of a true communal home!** By becoming self-sufficient, we reduce the need for huge chunks of the service economy geared—basically—just to support ourselves in an elaborate self-perpetuating matrix. Think for a minute of all the clothing stores that could be eliminated if we knew how to sew for ourselves. Working from home also lowers the need for so many restaurants, gas stations, and daycare centers, which are geared mainly to support an away-from-home workforce. We are on an ***infrastructure overload*** largely because of what the home and homeowner fall just shy of being able to achieve on their own.

Apart from lowering our environmental impact, the principles for having a home business are rather straightforward. We tend to work more productively at home, less travel is involved, we are able to spend more time with family, and there is enough savings in travel expenses to pay for the industrial-quality features we need to make it work. Better products can be made and we'd realize a trustworthy quality of service not seen in this country since the 1950s. There is the enjoyment of doing what you love the most, and there is also a lessened dependency on outside employment, which may fluctuate more in the future.

Completing the Home as a System

Being able to work from home completes the home as a system: supporting residents not just for 15 hours a day, but for the entire day! Expanding the home's performance just this little extra bit (on a community-wide scale) is what can create such cascading effects, leaving very little outside the home that we need. Indeed, the home is the ultimate arbiter of our fate and the key focal point at which our technological know-how must be fully applied.

Once such a conceptual foundation for working at home is established, we can basically ride these features up to larger and larger homes to realize an even greater economy of scale. Not only would larger facilities benefit residents by offering greater activity and living areas to enjoy, they would even begin to benefit their surrounding communities. Law firms, medical clinics, and even veterinarian offices can all be incorporated. All of the small one-story office buildings that are currently scattered throughout our communities would give way to one-stop-shopping (and one-stop-living for that matter) at its best!

Efficiency would <u>truly</u> be here to stay!

Chapter Five

Shared Common Areas:
The High-Powered Living Areas of Larger Homes

There is nothing else quite like communal living to allow our homes to concentrate the energies of otherwise humdrum features into truly high-powered living areas. By blending like features together and bringing them up to an astonishing level of completeness, we can easily create living, recreation, and work areas with **industrial, commercial,** and **professional** qualities! Restaurants begin to emerge from the resources that would have otherwise been poured into many wasteful individual kitchens. Research centers emerge from half-organized, third-bedroom workstations, and dedicated exercise rooms emerge from what would have separately amounted to only scattered pieces of exercise equipment stuck under people's beds. The top performance of such professional features (all listed out below) will gradually become more and more complete as the homes we design get larger. By the end of this chapter, we will see the potential benefit for communal homes as large as 10 to 21 stories, with the equivalent residential capacity of several hundred homes in some cases.

Restaurant-Quality Kitchens

The extended-family home design, as well as the larger multifamily homes, rode their performance levels up, largely on the strength of the modern kitchen. Dual in-wall ovens, 26-cubic-foot refrigerators, chest freezers, and five-burner stovetops, all allowed the residential capacity of these homes to be increased up to 32 in the one design. If we are to successfully exceed this limit in still larger multi-residential facilities, we will need to employ a newer commercial kitchen that will make feeding 48 + seem like a summer barbecue.

In place of what would amount to dozens of separate refrigerators in different homes, we would use a more efficient walk-in refrigerator and freezer unit. The size of these metal-lined units, typical of any restaurant, is about that of a small bedroom and can be built to suit the needs of any size facility. A restaurant-quality automatic dishwasher with stainless steel counters and 18-inch-deep pot-scrubbing sinks would be used. Salad bars would emerge from the equivalent of dozens of breakfast bars. Entire storage pantries would also emerge from many smaller kitchen closets.

Restaurant-Like Dining Rooms

Dining rooms of all sizes can feature top-quality four- to six-person leather seating booths, which themselves are **65**% smaller than a regular dining room and yet can be far more comfortable. For those who like to eat dinner more privately, there could be outward-facing seating arrangements. This arrangement uses a long table facing an array of bay windows. Instead of being huddled around one large table, you could sit individually and look outside to enjoy the day as you ate at your own pace. These three-foot-wide seats would also have partial privacy dividers separating them.

The dining room would be a soothing, low-light area with small overhead reading lights built-in over every table. Hardwood shelving units would also be built-in overhead. This would optimize normally wasted space and give the room a less boxy appearance. Such overhead units could hold office supplies, which help to support the potential research application of the dining area during off hours. Such overheads would also have video bars with multiple televisions to show multiple sporting events and news broadcasts. Each individual table and booth would be fully wired for laptop computers so that you can watch movies, read, or play music through a set of headphones while eating or just relaxing after hours. Valuable floor space would <u>not</u> be wasted on needless china cabinets that are typically just used as decorations and to fill space.

In general, such dining rooms take a more "come and go as you please" approach to dining, instead of a more traditional "it's time to sit down and eat" approach. We are all different. We all eat at different times, and many of us like to eat and quickly get right back to what we were doing. In order to break away from the typical circular table, on which food is set out and passed around, we also need to provide a buffet-style serving counter where people could get their plates and take what they wanted before they sat down.

Four to Six Preplanned Dining Periods

Having a dining room that is large enough to hold every resident and visitor in the home would be ***extremely*** wasteful! It usually doesn't take much more than 25 minutes for most people to eat their dinner. In a multi-residential home—where you can work from home and eat whenever you want—people wouldn't be forced into such a narrow dinnertime schedule as they are today. With this in mind, I am emphatic about using smaller dining areas that only have one-fourth to one-sixth the capacity that would be needed to hold every resident and visitor. This means that it would take at least four back-to-back 30-minute dining periods for everyone to sit down and eat (at maximum capacity). That would be from, say, 4:30 to 6:30 in the evenings and 6:30 to 8:30 in the mornings. Times well within most people's eating habits. Eating before or after these periods is certainly fine and would help lessen the crowd during peak times. The possible use of multiple work shifts within the home can also help spread things out. Structured dining periods might seem like an inconvenience, but this single arrangement (easily possible through proper planning) is vital if we are to make room available for things like an 8,000-volume library, an 84-seat home movie theater, and an indoor racquetball court. Even on a small scale, the 12-place dining room in **Figure 16 (Page 49)** uses <u>85</u>% less volume than what an equivalent number of single-family homes would have used!

Separated Living Areas

A contemporary dining room typically sits between an open living room and an open kitchen. This open-air arrangement is an ***unforgivable fault*** in a home's layout, which allows any noise in any one area to disturb the entire section. Washing dishes can disturb those watching television. The television can be disturbing to those eating or trying to study in the dining room. And the smell of something burning in the kitchen is also transmitted throughout the home. These problems may not be noticeable in a single-family home, but they certainly would be in a communal home.

To allow these areas to be used for separate activities simultaneously, we need to separate them. Not only does this add more wall length for the placement of furniture and lower noise levels throughout the home, it is structurally more stable and prevents a storm-damaged wall or window from adversely affecting the entire home. It prevents the rapid spread of fire and smoke and allows unused rooms to be closed off, conserving the heat or air-conditioning. We can further separate the pantry storage area from the main kitchen to prevent people busy restocking shelves from interfering with the home's cooking staff.

The typical placement of the home's front door in the main living room is another unforgivable fault of a typical home's layout and is why we go to so much trouble to make the living room so formal. This is why we then have to rely on other den areas for more casual use. Having the home's front door enter into a mudroom (complete with a coat rack and bench seats) is a much more functional and much less disturbing option.

The Pool Table Game Room/Sports Bar

Apart from the use of the home's restaurant-quality dining room as a nightclub after hours, active residents will find the home's first-rate game room/sports bar a rewarding and pleasurable experience. Combined and highly consolidated from what would have been dozens of underutilized, often incomplete, and cluttered basement rec. rooms, these game rooms could alternate between teen and adults-only nights. As for a place to watch the playoffs while shooting pool and socializing, nothing would compare to its wall-mounted plasma monitors and its professional sound system. Booth seating is provided in larger designs. A nearby walk-in conversion closet containing a table tennis, air hockey, and card table **(Figure 27 – Page 60)**, allows the game room to occasionally swap out the pool table for other games. Temporarily converting the entire room into a living area is also an option.

Home Movie Theater/Conference Center

In a day and age of such amazing science fiction and action movies and equally wonderful science and history documentaries, we would be rather remiss not to have a state-of-the-art home movie theater: one not just with surround-sound, but with Sensoround! Did anyone see Midway when it was out in Sensoround? I nearly pissed my pants! I was only nine… Watching Jaws and Salem's Lot at about that same age was probably not such a good idea. Home theaters, which can range in size from a well-equipped den to one with 140 seats or more, help to bring the power of this art to its rightful place. Such a room would also be great for holding seminars and weeklong conferences, and because it is <u>our</u> home, we can opt for extra wide leather bucket seating. Popcorn anyone?

Shops, Offices, Project, and Craft Rooms

As mentioned, high-performance cabinet and furniture shops would emerge from combining all the scattered workbenches found in smaller single-family homes. Large craft rooms are also provided in my designs so that a group of residents can get together to work on hobbies, such as pottery, macramé, quilting, knitting, sewing, and basket weaving. These are things everyone can enjoy, especially with the encouragement and help of others! In the last two designs, we also started to see the use of modest 9 x 12 (2.7 x 3.6 m) project rooms which serve as more specialized and individualized offices, writing or design labs, art rooms, model building areas, and so on.

Although the individual offices found in these homes are mainly intended to generate income from customers as various private practices, many such practices can also benefit the home's residents during off hours.

Fully Featured Health and Fitness Areas

For eight years I trained in the martial arts. I learned Modern Arnis, kung fu, Tai Chi, and yoga. Because of the popularity of these activities, multi-residential facilities will feature a large, open training area for sparring and conducting classes in. Such a school could be used for various seminars and receptions when needed.

A vital, irreplaceable part of such training involves the use of heavy bags to kick and punch into, so that you develop your joints to be able to hit into something strongly. Training rooms for heavy punching bags and various striking dummies, as well as a weight room (for both strengthening and rehabilitation) and stretching areas, are all important for effective training and conditioning.

Because hitting into a punching bag can be very noisy, specific punching bag rooms are hard to design into a home. In the first three homes we saw, residents were forced to do such training either outdoors or in the garage. In **Figure 23 (Page 56),** the training room is located in the basement where it is far away from other living areas.

A true multi-residential home can be truly exceptional, given the quality and number of the sports-related activity areas it incorporates: features that no one would ever expect to find in most small communities, let alone in an individual home:

- A rooftop tennis/basketball/volleyball court (enclosed on the sides like a courtyard) that can be used for just about any activity you can think of **(Figure 43 – Page 99).** It could serve as a roller-blade hockey rink, used for playing Frisbee and catch, for outdoor parties and concerts, and for Tai Chi classes. Through the use of an inexpensive inflatable cover, the entire rooftop could be used year-round.
- An indoor 20 x 40 racquetball/walleyball court that could alternate as a 20-foot-high gymnastics-training center **(Figure 27 – Page 60).**
- An exercise/weight room with treadmills, exercise bikes, stair climbers, rowing and ski machines, and a multipurpose weightlifting home gym.
- A rehabilitation room for the elderly or disabled (with whirlpool and massage table).
- A climbing wall incorporated right onto the outside face of the building itself.

Outdoor Activity Support

When we take what would normally amount to some personal hiking, camping, fishing, climbing, and biking gear (which is typically stored away in many boxes throughout the home) and we combine all of it together, we realize an entirely new feature in the home: a camping center. Pristine gear racks, a bike repair and modification shop, and a ready-up area near the home's rear entrance, would allow residents who love the outdoors to have a great time. Such a center is proportional to the extreme usefulness and diversity of modern camping gear and all the various portable electronics that are now available. Such top-quality equipment, like GPS and multifunctional two-way radios, will be efficiently shared by residents as needed.

Camping centers are also important given the widespread availability of edible wild plants. Perhaps as much as 50% of the everyday weeds and trees you see are edible in some way at some point. Many came from Europe, where they were grown as regular vegetables. They are just as edible, recognizable, and often better tasting, than most of the vegetables you are familiar with. These hardy plants provide much more nutrition than store-bought vegetables because they can be eaten within minutes as opposed to days "by which time many nutrients have already been dissolved."[10] Armed with various field guides, I was able to identify about 70 such plants in Central Pennsylvania in just a couple months' time.

State-of-the-Art Computer Systems

Individual computers give us access to data from around the world. Data storage disks have also become highly capacious, enabling just a few to hold what is currently housed in the Library of Congress. Computer software is available for many applications. Word processors far outperform typewriters. Spreadsheets and databases can organize and access data in numerous ways, and there is software to help you edit photographs, draw, and design just about anything. AutoCAD, for example, is a $7,000 software package used by businesses to create three-dimensional drawings. Anything from a submarine to jumbo-jets can be designed and even tested using this software.

To support the use of such software, businesses use a central server-style computer system. Servers are industrial-strength desktop computers that other computers are linked to. Because of their importance, servers are almost always decked out with the best features available. They typically have a set of dual-processing chips, up to ten hard drives, and 30 times the RAM of an ordinary PC.[11]

All of the computers within the network can execute any software that is stored on the server, which can be several hundred other computers: saving money on expensive software. Such powerful software and the performance to run it can definitely help us to establish more extensive home-based businesses. The combined purchasing power that is only available in a communal home will make the server (and those still more advanced computers that follow) and the most powerful business-related software packages accessible to the public-at-large for the first time.

---

[10] Field Guide to Edible Wild Plants by Bradford Angier
[11] Gail Cooper – June 2000

A Dedicated Electronics/Computer Room

The server will be housed in a special computer room, along with a host of other commercial-quality electronics. Instead of having many small desktop printers in each home, for example, the computer room will house a single color printer/copy machine (about the size of a bedroom dresser) with the speed to support our businesses and our research activities. A single fax machine and a few flatbed scanners can also serve the needs of the entire household and can be replaced much more economically with newer, more up-to-date models than many individual units. The electronics/computer room will also have a large fire safe as well as office supply cabinets.

Generally, the computer room should not be located along an outer wall of the home so that it is protected from possible storm damage. To protect delicate electronics, the walls would be thicker, protected from water damage, and perhaps even lined with a layer of copper to protect electronics from an electromagnetic flux (EMP) weapon.

Fully Featured Research Center

Does such computer capability warrant having a home office? Is a corner desk in the living room or in the spare bedroom adequate for conducting this level of research? When we come together to secure our economic concerns and have generated a third more free time for ourselves, we will have a need, not just for a small office, but a fully featured research facility! The library and computer are just tools. Our perception, observations, and cognizance are forces within reality itself.[12] Learning truly honors our self-awareness and is implied in our very existence.

A multi-residential home's highly customized research center will be soundproof and contain audio and video systems that are just as much a part of the intense levels of research we conduct as the computer systems themselves. Alternating between dead quiet and deafening concert-level sound to suit the changing intensity of the atmosphere, this room is designed to keep us poised on the edge of the moment, seeking its subtleties and gripping realism. Six-speaker, high-fidelity stereo systems would carry the thundering 300-watt emotionally charged heavy metal songs like ***"Widowmaker"*** and ***"Blood Red Skies,"*** which impart a tremendous sense of urgency in what we are doing.[13] Video systems help to add direction to our efforts by bringing a sense of realism to what we see and how we see it: the Zebruder film played back and then forward, the realism of combat, the gravity of events, or the study of any issue that merely reading about could not hope to convey the truths we seek.

Highly comfortable furniture will facilitate intense 18-hour days. Computer and board gaming tables (which can help us generate theoretical models and test concepts) would be available. There may be a specific design-denoting counter in the room used to gather changes and ideas we need to apply to the products we manufacture. Completed research, which can include everything from information-filled-binders to model displays and artifacts, may have its own special area. Customized computer workstations throughout would have multiple monitors, reflecting not only the many facets of an intense project but

---

[12] Tao of Physics
[13] Wasp – 1985/Judas Priest – 1988

also the person's tastes and interests. Some monitors may be built into a conforming console that wraps around and between individualized workstations, perhaps more reminiscent of a cockpit than an office.

In support of such a research center, there may be several project rooms that serve as writing, art, and designing labs. Such areas could be tasked with building on or finalizing a project and then packaging it into different formats to suit the needs of different publications. The equal intensity of a group debate can be facilitated in a side conference room, which may have recording equipment so nothing is lost.

Interior Decorating

To provide an atmosphere conducive to communal living, we would call on the art and science of interior decorators to provide the appropriate color contrasts and lighting for such functionally laid out, compact, and high-intensity homes. A combination of blue and white is calming, for example, and is a subtle way of keeping the edge off our emotions. We can also employ such things as highly advanced E-paper wallpaper that can actually change its color and pattern to match the time of day, the seasons, or the particular tastes of the people in the room. Racecars and rocket ships may be the theme when it's the younger children's turn to use the game room, and sports and rock posters the theme when the teenagers use it.

A General-Area Sound System

Using a Muzak sound system in the home adds privacy by providing a light backdrop of sound. Because sound is one of the main privacy concerns in a communal home, we need to use this tool to tastefully drown out some of the things you can't avoid overhearing. Bedroom hallways, for example, can have soft ocean sounds or acoustic guitar solos. Louder, thundering music can be played in and among the bathroom toilet stalls! In any event, when you get to pick the music and where it gets played (thus maintaining individuality), you'll find this to be a remarkable tool to maintain privacy.

Muzak stereo systems are also the industrial giants of the stereo world. They can have a 300-CD capacity and be a 100-watt hi-fi unit! They're about the size of a small bedroom nightstand and would be placed in the home's electronics/computer room.

Home Schooling Class and Conference Rooms

In a day and age of school violence, drugs, and teen pornography, we literally have to fight to protect our children. Public schools are failing to produce children that have any real desire to learn. At home (where at least a few residents should have teaching degrees), we can teach our children more correctly and much faster than public schools. Imagine having children who can speak three languages by the time they're 14, or having them move through a college textbook on their own!

In smaller homes, research areas, craft shops, and conference rooms make excellent classrooms, especially when adults are at work. In larger multi-residential homes, however, specific home schooling classrooms would be needed. In the evenings, such classrooms can be easily converted into children's play areas.

70

A Home Library

One community of 90 people I visited had more than 10,000 books, not to mention an extensive music and magazine collection. When we start to think about combining this vast repository of knowledge, we can easily see the need for a home library. Having a library, much like having a camping center and project rooms, is just a more active place to store belongings that we may not quite have enough room for in our own bedroom. Residents would be given bookshelves of their own, but from which other people can easily borrow. Sign-out sheets, indexes, and accurately labeled shelves would keep such arrangements well organized.

One of the best ways I've found to incorporate a library into a home is to line the otherwise wasted walls of a hallway with glass paneled shelving units. Not only do these wider hallways provide access to the books without having to dedicate a small room to them, it also creates a much more pleasant atmosphere, where a mixture of books, collectibles, and model displays line ordinary, humdrum hallways **(Figure 41 – Page 97 – right side).**

Corporate Telephone Systems

All of my homes will be equipped with the very latest corporate telephone systems: ones able to provide <u>everyone</u> with their own outside line and voice mailbox. These electronic voicemail systems can perform the function of hundreds of individual answering machines with a single control box. Such a voicemail system can be accessed from outside the home, allowing vacationers to keep up on all of their messages. People can forward recorded messages to another person, personalize their voicemail greeting, and even overlay such a greeting with a temporary message to let callers know they are away.

Callers to the home's main number can be greeted by an automated system that directs calls to specific areas; you know the ones: *"Please press 1 for Harry's Towing Service."* Or, *"Your call is important to us... please stay on the line and a representative will be with you shortly."* It is at this time (while the caller is stuck on hold) that we can mischievously play heavy metal songs (loaded with subliminal messages about purchasing our products), instead of Barry Manilow tunes that make them too lethargic to spend their money.

These corporate telephones also have conference call features and speakerphones to allow up to six telephones in six separate locations to be conferenced together. Other options include hold, transfer, multiple speed dial settings, and headsets can be used so that you can continue to work productively while you talk. To avoid having to physically find someone somewhere in the building, you can also use the speakerphone as a system-wide intercom to page them.

The inability to find people when someone called on a regular phone was a major problem at one community. They never would actually answer the phone when it rang "because it often meant you would have to go all over hunting for someone!"[14] In general, these newer phone systems with such advanced capabilities have never before been available. They increase the quality of life for individual users, and they allow such large communal homes as we are talking about here to functionally exist for the first time!

---

[14] Twin Oaks visitors liaison – May 1999

Soundproof Music Room

To facilitate any person's desire to play and learn a music instrument (other than, say, a trumpet), we need soundproof music rooms that are located well away from other areas **(Figure 23 – Page 56).** PC-based digital recording equipment will be available to use, and an actual recording room will be added to larger designs. Apart from an array of electronics, a recording room would have an internal bay window through which producers can insist that musicians be more polite to their instruments during yet another retake. As *'Mytheril Multimedia Ministries'* of Marysville, Pennsylvania (not to be confused with Dan's Bar & Grill) demonstrated (when they produced, cut, mixed, and mastered a CD of Celtic instrumentals from within a 64-square-foot corner of a basement), you don't need a lot of room or capital to send an exceptional work of art down the vast corridor of time.[15]

Customized Furniture

The appalling numbers we saw earlier that showed how little we actually use the home's various activity areas are further compounded by the fact that most people furnish their homes as if to just decorate them. Decorative nightstands and end tables do little more than support a table lamp. Entertainment centers, a bedroom's chest of drawers and armoire, and other contemporary shelving units have 25% to 75% less usable area than built-in furnishings that run floor-to-ceiling. Thus, the rooms of a home are not only infrequently used and only half used when they are, we also only get about half as much performance as we can out of them because of their poor storage capacity.

To improve this, upward of 85% of the home's furniture will be built-in. Wall-to-wall, floor-to-ceiling hardwood furnishings (manufactured in our own cabinetry shops) will provide higher performance and quality than mass-produced furnishings. Bookcases built right into the wall would not have shelves that sag. Shelves would be deeper than normal so that they can hold model and collectable displays. The lip of each shelf can be raised slightly to prevent valuables from vibrating off. Lighting and glass cabinet doors would be added.

More customized items that are just not available anywhere else could also be added to the home for greater efficiency of use. Instead of having to get down and root through a crowded lower-level kitchen cabinet for your favorite soft drink, for example, we could manufacture a unique countertop lazy susan specially designed for about a dozen two-liter soda bottles. With even a bit of swagger in our unbroken walk passed the **'soda susan'**, which we could apply a slightly more than gracious spin to, we could grab a soft drink and (after getting a glass and proceeding to the icemaker) be out of everybody's way in no time. Basically, whenever people find themselves running into contention with one another or having to struggle with something, instead of getting angry, they should ask if there's a design solution to the problem. Most often there is!

The home's wardrobe rooms would also benefit from custom-made cabinetry, too. They would have top shelves that are a foot deeper than we normally see. This makes use of <u>all</u> the space above a clothing hang bar, not just part of it. The one drawback to such an extensive use of customized, built-in furnishings will be the need for large bulk storage areas for the furniture that people owned before they moved in.

---

[15] Darrell Troutman – summer of 1999

Specialized, High-Performance Bathrooms

In order to consolidate plumbing and prevent people seeking to use the bathroom from having to hunt for an open toilet to use, we need to combine widely separated single-seat bathrooms into larger men's and women's specific office-style bathroom facilities: ones with separate toilet stalls, shower, and sink areas. Individual toilet stalls would be wider and deeper than normal. They would also be completely enclosed without a gap under the door or side partitions, almost like a half bathroom but without the sink. Having, say, three toilet stalls in a bathroom is actually like having three bathrooms side-by-side.

The sinks in these office-style bathrooms are partitioned off from one another and indented enough so that people washing their hands or brushing their teeth do not block access in and out of the bathroom. The water-free urinal in the men's room would sit in a deep, fully partitioned off indent with its own privacy curtain. Having a urinal is like having an extra toilet, and there is no contamination of a toilet seat to contend with. One urinal is usually more than plenty. Some toilets (as we have seen) will be composting toilets, which are water-free. The others will either be the American Standard low-flush Champion or liquefying toilets (called the Fluidizer), which use a small propeller to liquefy solid waste and that flush using only a third the water that a low-flush toilets use.[16] ADA (Americans with Disabilities Act) compliant shower stalls, which are extra large (39 x 39 inches), would themselves be partitioned off from the rest of the bathroom. This further reduces the number of times that people would find the bathroom occupied and inaccessible.

Bathrooms will have a wonderful new floor-covering system that is specially coated with a nontoxic, antibacterial compound developed by Toto Kiki. The coating consists of titanium oxide and copper, which react with light and air to overexpose bacteria to oxygen. These floors, placed in a high-use public facility, "showed no mildew, even after being left un-cleaned for nine months."[17] Such advanced systems are again employed to help the home and its residents cope under such a heightened degree of usage.

Included in the home's plumbing subsystems are a rooftop gravity-fed water tank, backup wellheads, and separate plumbing systems, used to capture relatively clean water (gray water) from showers and sinks. This water can then be run through a simple filtering system (called the Aquasaver) and sent back into the home to flush the toilets with.

A Bank Vault and Security Station

Multi-residential homes may have a vault to protect important documents and valuables. The number of people in some homes would warrant having a vault about the same size that an ordinary bank has, and we will see this in the next home design **(Figure 32 – Page 87)**. Residents can store insurance policies and wills, certificates, and valuables in the vault, where they will be secure until needed. A vault may be incorporated into the home along side an actual security station. Having an actual security station in the home may be essential, depending on what types of businesses we operate. Video cameras are needed to monitor customer areas as well as the front door because visitors come and go more freely than they do in single-family homes.

---

[16] Popular Science – March 1994
[17] Popular Mechanics "Light Powers Antibacterial Tile"

Chapter Summary

The culmination of all of these full-blown features from virtually nonexistent performance levels exemplifies the extraordinary benefits that can be gained through communal living. These features are in direct proportion to the number of residents living in the home and are representative of the fact that such features will certainly be used much more often. Single families living on their own have to balance what features they incorporate into their homes with what they can afford and what they are likely to use. These families will almost always pass up the chance to incorporate such features as we have seen here because, for how little they are likely to use them, it would not be worth it. Whereas a husband and wife probably wouldn't shoot a game of pool that often (if ever), a larger group of adults and children would be likely to play several times a week, if not several times a day. In exactly the same progression, with women doing their own things together, and the men doing guy-type things together, we can begin to see the need for features that most couples would find unheard of.

It is important to realize that the addition of all of these features into the home would not be proportional if—at the same time—we tried to have a substantial amount of personal space above and beyond having a private bedroom. In other words, we wouldn't want to provide each resident with a two-room suite (composed of a bedroom and a bedroom-sized living area) as well as features like a home gymnasium and a library. If we tried to have both, we'd only end up doubling the size of the home. Such extensive personal space would dilute the whole intended purpose for having such extensive activity areas. Thus, we'd be right back to a situation where the main living areas remained unoccupied 70% to 98% of the time, and under utilized when they were.

Doing things with others is fun!

Chapter Six

How Far Can Communal Living Be Taken?

In the last chapter, we established many features that would allow the home to be increased to virtually any size. Combining professional work facilities like a small medical clinic and veterinarian office, with such things as a restaurant and health club, literally gave these homes the diversity of services found in a modest community. When the proper subsystems exist and aesthetics have been put in their proper place, there is no reason to stop envisioning bigger homes with still greater benefits. The main objective in continually increasing the home's size like this is to get to a point where all features meet at an even/proportional level of completeness, before we reach the limits of what is practical. To this end, we first need to understand what constraints we are working against and also what new technology can be used to help us meet our goals. Achieving my goal of reducing society's impact by **98**% has required battling each constraint with still more progressive communal ways of organization, newer technology, and more functional floor plans that will truly allow people to live this way successfully!

Constraint 1 – Cost

At first, the primary constraint is obviously going to be cost. Multifamily homes and multi-residential buildings are extremely expensive, requiring the consistent financial participation of residents over several decades. Not only is a commercial-quality building more expensive to build but also the cost of having 85% of the home's furnishings custom-made is significant as well. It is critical, however, to use such high-quality furnishings if we are to get the performance we need from such a consolidated design.

Although it may seem immensely expensive to afford a home that has all the elaborate and high-quality features described above, it really isn't. As we saw in the cost breakdown on page 61, the savings that such a facility would realize on travel-related expenses, as well as on nursing home and daycare costs would virtually allow the home to pay for itself in 30 years. These savings would multiply continuously over the many decades and centuries that followed: something that always made me believe that a good home like this would literally be *cheap at twice the price!*

Constraint 2 – Finding the Right People

Another constraint involves how many people we can find to live with us. Newly forming communities certainly struggle just to get started. Thus, we must consider limits to the size and the number of features the home will have. In this sense, modular buildings that can be added to or finished off as more people become involved, may be the best way to compensate for limited starting funds and our desire for larger, more fully featured facilities. We could try to build in locations near existing communes or where the people are generally more open to the idea, such as in college towns or in places with a diversity of cultures. If we did have a well-organized group to start with, we would certainly be free to build larger, more fully featured units, but only up to a point.

Constraint 3 – Overall Size

No one is talking about building a communal skyscraper, but if we could, should we? Even if finances are not the problem, there are other constraints that demand that we be more reasonable. Even before 9/11, skyscrapers should have been considered a death trap, as no way was ever devised to evacuate people in the event of a fire. The chance of a fire, a natural disaster, a chemical spill nearby, a foundation problem, and even resale value are all things to consider. The infrastructure needed to support such a massive building is itself vulnerable to such problematic events. Thus, the overall size of the buildings we plan must be constrained to more reasonable levels.

With these potential disasters in mind, we should limit the height of any theoretical building we may plan to a maximum of 20 to 30 aboveground floors. In the design of such a home, there should be ample staircases for emergency use and perhaps even an emergency egress chute that elderly or disabled people can slide down. To protect the building and its occupants still further, powerful water cannons would take the place of ordinary fire hydrants near the base of the building. Such cannons don't have to wait for a fire truck to show up and can also be used to engage any wildfires that threaten the grounds.

Although not quite a constraint, there are several other concerns with building too large. Realizing that these are very pressing times and that even homes with 75% less land use than an equivalent number of single-family homes is too substantial to forgo, we need to begin building tens of thousands of these smaller and less expensive units to get things rolling. This does not preclude large units; it just acknowledges the need for substantial change early on. We need buildings that people can afford without searching endlessly for potential residents and that local contractors can build without too much trouble. Smaller multifamily homes also have a greater chance of working out at first because residents will know the people whom they are moving in with right from the start.

One important option to consider instead of building big is multiple building arrangements. A community may start out with a smaller 7-bedroom unit but save the ideal location on their property for a much larger facility. Communities starting out with a great many interested people may choose to build two side-by-side homes instead of a massive unit that would take longer to build and put more resources at risk should something bad happen. In such a plan, there would be an inherent flexibility regarding personnel arrangements, allowing people of similar interests to group together more.

Constraint 4 – Environmental Considerations

On top of the above constraints, we must now design a building that will be literally shoehorned onto the smallest possible plot of land! Our responsibility to the environment not only dictates that we build over previously used (perhaps even unwanted) land, but that we do so with as small a footprint as possible. Even if North America were still covered by virgin forests, we would still want to be vigilant about how much land we used, if not even more so. Although we may not be seeking a 30-story apartment tower, multistory buildings are too easy to construct to be disregarded, simply because of their added expense or a general view of being somehow "unnatural" or "cold." Adding even a third or fourth level to a structure would be a significant savings. Building completely over a multilevel parking garage is critical, since parking lots invariably take up more land than the actual buildings do. Utilizing the space under the driveway and actually planting dense juniper gardens on as much of the rooftop and driveway overhang as possible (a concept called a living rooftop) is also important to save and utilize land effectively.

The added structural qualities that are inherent in a taller, commercial-quality building would be well worth their added expense regardless. The quality of construction and the durability of any building can be considered an important environmental factor because the longer a building lasts, the less it will have to be torn down, disposed of, and rebuilt. A commercial building suffers less damage from hurricanes and other potential disasters than individual homes or trailers do. The newest, non-rusting steels and concrete used to construct these buildings are relatively invulnerable to fires or pervasive insects, and they don't rot out over time like wooden-framed homes. Durability and longevity are stabilizing factors that not only allow a home to weather a severe storm, but to also survive long enough after being paid for to benefit our grandchildren.

Building a home the very best we can, perhaps one able to last upwards of a thousand years, would certainly be a wise investment. Although building a home to last such extraordinary amounts of time is unheard of, this isn't science fiction. The Seattle Superdome was a contemporary structure designed to last such a duration of time. As long as the heating, cooling, and electronic systems of such facilities are replaceable, we are justified in building the best possible residential dwelling that we can. We need to achieve our potential, not languish a penny wise but dollar foolish.

Constraint 5 – Efficiency

Environmental and cost concerns are not only factors in the building of the home, but also factors in its operation. Buildings must be ultra efficient to save money. Using less power prevents excess pollution caused by coal-burning power companies and all of the open strip mining involved with obtaining coal. How cost-effective it will be to run a building can even be a precursor to building it. If you can't afford to run it, why build it? The less a building costs to run, the less we'll have to travel to earn the money we need to support it; thus, the impact of travel on the environment and the costs associated that become part of the equation, cascading still further.

The need for ultra-efficiency is a constraint that restricts us to a select few designs that have a low surface area, which transfers less heat into the building in the summer months and lets less heat escape in the winter. As we saw in the case of my mom's townhouse, which had <u>half</u> the electric heating bills of her previous home, any combined building will have far less surface area than many smaller ones: in her case, 36.6% less. We also saw how just by changing from an inefficient rectangular-shaped townhouse to a square one with a flat roof, it was possible to reduce surface area by an additional 7.8%. Other shapes like cylinders **(Figure 28)** and spheres have the lowest amount of surface area for a given volume but are terribly hard to build correctly, requiring a custom frame not unlike an aircraft. Spheres and domes (although entirely possible) use way too much land because they are broadest at their base as well. As we have seen in two previous designs, octagonal shapes are strong, wind resistant (a much needed key for taller buildings), easier to build, and very close (within 3%) to a cylinder's highly efficient shape.

The most important thing to remember is that the percentage of surface area is most dramatically lowered with an increase in size—provided, of course, that we don't ruin this advantage by trying to make the structure stylish or fancy in any way. Townhouses might sound efficient, but consider, if you will, that the next seven-story, square communal home, will have <u>70%</u> less external surface area than 27 separate homes, not just 36.6% less. Such a building would have one-fourth the heat transfer! Because the exterior surface of any home is composed of more expensive materials (such as thicker walls, more insulation, windows, and, in the case of the outer walls, the more expensive foundation they sit on), a reduction in surface area can also reduce a home's initial cost, as well as the cost of any future repairs.

Making Use of Advanced Materials and High Technology

Much like it is essential to know what constraints we face, we also need to understand what we have to work with. We are, literally, in a day and age of utterly incomprehensible technology. There are alloys known as liquid metal, alloys that do not rust, and now even concrete that bends **(Figure 37 – Page 93).**[18] Liquid metal, for example, is a solid that has *"twice the strength-to-weight ratio of titanium."*[19] It's an extremely hard metal within which the process of crystallization has been prevented by rapidly freezing the mold. The crystallization process in other metals can also be manipulated by freezing one end of a molten casting, so that a single crystal grows from one end to the other. This creates high strength and much greater heat tolerance, which can be critical in preventing a building's collapse in the event of a fire. Could you imagine having the main structural support beams of the home built of these exotic metals and how long it would last? Reinforcement bars that do not rust are also essential for use within concrete to prevent its eventual decay.

Apart from exotic metals, there is also a revolution going on in plastic materials called composites. They are not only lighter than aluminum but also stronger than steel. There are also advanced materials that absorb sound much better than in the past, which have obvious applications in a communal home. There are anti-noise systems, which generate acoustic signals to cancel out unwanted noise. Such advanced levels of soundproofing would permit a more compact arrangement, where one large building consolidates the features of many. In this day and age, even window glass and insulation are high-tech!

---

[18] Popular Science – February 1991
[19] Popular Mechanics – July 1998

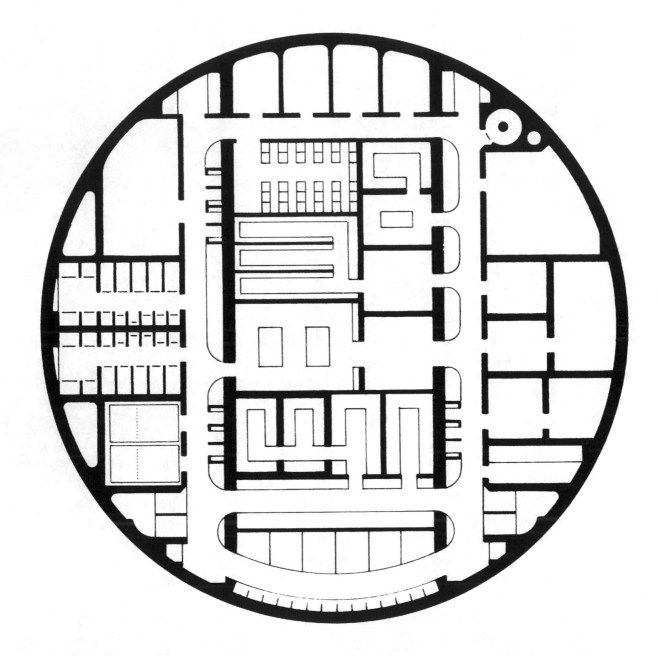

Figure 28 – The Recreation level of an 11-story 36-meter-diameter communal dwelling:

Clockwise from top – around the outside: Four age-oriented living rooms. Observation area with PC counter. A circular emergency egress chute. A PC research den/classroom. Three home schooling classrooms with alternate research applications during evening hours. Two music rooms and one recording room. A staircase. An observation area with trash receptacle. At bottom, a 40-seat dining room/nightclub with six contoured dining booths. An observation area with trash receptacle. A staircase. Dual elevators. Men's and women's five-stall bathrooms (flanked by ventilation and plumbing shafts). Health club/weight room. Observation area with seat.

Center Area: The four side-by-side rooms across the bottom are the home's kitchen facilities. There are a walk-in freezer (far left), a walk-in refrigerator, a kitchen, and a dishwashing room (far right). These rooms support a long steam table aisle with snack and beverage counters just below them. Above these rooms (up the left-hand side) are a two-pool table game room, a 19,000-volume library, and a 30-seat movie theater/conference center. Running up the right side is a conversion closet (for extra parlor games and musical instruments), a reading room, a conference room, and an office/server computer room.

Advanced Mechanical and Computer Subsystems

Apart from such phenomenal materials and an industrial know-how that could build just about anything, technology is fast galvanizing its strength in creating mechanical and electrical systems for the home that will truly enable it to meet the needs of its residents. There are automation systems, advanced air and water filtration systems, various heating and cooling concepts, and certainly many ways for the home to generate its own power.

Much like advanced heating, cooling, and other mechanical systems, the home's plumbing and ventilation systems have to be absolutely top-notch to hold up to the expected workload found in a building pressing toward the theoretical edge of what is possible. Oversized plumbing, sprinkler, and air-conditioning systems function much like the circulatory and respiratory systems of a long-distance runner, breathing life into the home. These systems are maintained through the use of strategically placed access conduits and crawlways that are vertical and horizontal access junctions hidden in walls and floors. To accommodate these access conduits (as well as ventilation duct work), the floors of the home need to be three feet thick, with framing that would facilitate the placement of these services and crawlways. Plumbing should be as consolidated as possible as well. This is necessary because it saves having to run the water as long to get hot water, it lowers the initial cost of plumbing, and it will make repair and replacement simpler. To accommodate this need, the placement of the bathrooms and washing machines, in relation to the hot water heaters, becomes very important.

Computers also have a decisive role to play in the home's subsystems: managing the home's internal mechanical and electrical systems. For homes the size that we are talking about, the computer's ability to monitor environmental conditions and automate countless individual functions could prove to be a key factor in making communal life that much more possible and trouble free. Homes can be automated in a number of ways. Large and complex environmental systems are a particular area of importance. Through a series of sensors, computers can monitor and adjust heating, cooling, humidifying and dehumidifying, ion, ozone, and filtration settings throughout the home. The temperature settings in the garage can be increased in anticipation of routine daily use, and so on. Motorized windows at key areas can be opened to regulate internal and external temperature differences automatically. The water system can be monitored for pressure irregularities that could cause damage or which may indicate a leak or an open valve somewhere in the system. Overdraws on power can be rerouted to a heavier circuit, faulty switches can be detected, and backup generators instantly engaged during a power fluctuation.

Fire and security systems can also benefit from a home automation system. If an alarm were triggered, such a system would indicate what part of the system was tripped, so that people knew what was happening and what areas to avoid. Positive identification systems will be used in many areas, especially around places like the server computer room and vault/security section. Computers can even monitor customers through a video system and ID a criminal in the FBI database via new face recognition software that can even see through disguises.[20] Do you see how all these systems make so much more possible?

---

[20] Popular Mechanics – June 1997

Chapter Summary

Although we may have initially thought the sheer cost of such large, high-performance homes would be our biggest limitation, it actually was not the leading factor. What type of home we can afford to build is directly proportional to how many individuals and families—longing for more stability, security, and free time—we can find to take part in such an involved project. The more people that can be drawn together, the larger and more complete the home being planned can become. The number of potential residents we can find is itself directly relational to the quality, performance, and completeness of the home's features and layout, its location, and the professionalism of the residents who are planning the project. Having a model home that people can see may be the deciding factor in many cases. People planning a home with a full suite of work facilities, professional kitchens, and an 8,000-volume library, that is scenically located, and that has the financial backing of several well-established professionals, can count on generating **A LOT** of interest!

This sort of ***cascading/self-feeding loop*** between the number and quality of residents we can find and the increased size and high-performance features of the home that attracts them is directly influenced by another factor: our environmental and ultra-efficiency directives. To these two directives, the home simply could not be large enough! Not only would such facilities use between $1/3^{rd}$ and $1/50^{th}$ the amount of land as single-family homes, they would lessen if not eliminate the impact of travel on the environment, and they will eventually decrease the number of supportive services needed throughout a community. Most people have a serious concern for the environment but up until now have been at a loss as to what to do. In this regard, the home's extreme environmentally friendly status and its ultra-efficiency allow us to attract still more potential residents and, thus again, build still larger homes with still more attractive features. The high technology of various mechanical and electrical subsystems that ordinary home owners can't afford can also be put into place and replaced much more easily as upgrades are made to keep these systems at their peak, further increasing efficiency. Basically, with very little in the way to limit us, we can push the bounds of what is currently thought possible!

It is for these various reasons that this book offers not only homes for small beginner groups and homes for well-organized professionals, but also truly monolithic units that are best termed as theoretical models at this time. Such models are critical, however! We need to always know what is one step further, even if it were just to see what it would be like. Only when we know what's next can we decide for ourselves if it is worth trying to fight for.

In a way, it is sort of like playing the *"what-if"* game. What if we had the commitment of huge corporations or government grants behind us? What if zillions of people were standing in line to get into these places? What if we won the lottery? We'd be negligent if we didn't at least provide such models to look at. To this extent, the developmental home designs I'm about to present may not be entirely realistic or even largely practical right now. However, they are well worth at least thinking about and improving upon until the time comes that they are needed. We need to be ready to go when the time comes. Joe Public could surprise even the most optimistic planners when he gets something in his head,

wanting it yesterday!

Chapter Seven

The Multi-Residential Homes of Tomorrow

Right from the start, we established that the main personal requirement for living communally was to gain more than we are giving up. At first, communal living seems like an outright conflict of interest. Traditionally, the home is viewed as a place for quiet relaxation and living a private life with close loved ones; thus, the presence of other people would surely degrade the home's whole intended purpose. Right? For communal living to even come close to making such shared arrangements acceptable, many detailed changes had to be made to the layout of the home. Kitchens, dining rooms, and living areas had to all be separated to prevent activities in one area from adversely affecting all the other adjoining areas. Kids' rooms, as well as specific music, craft, and exercise rooms, had to be added to a communal home in order to replace the single-family home's ability to use its general living areas for these activities. There had to be greater bedroom privacy and ample storage space for couples to consolidate all of their personal belongings, which no longer could be kept throughout the home in various closets and end table drawers. Larger hot water heaters, an elevator, wider hallways, and a multi-line phone system were needed. And, bathrooms also had to be adapted to the demands of such intensified living conditions. Basically, there are a lot of enhancements needed in a communal home that can just be disregarded in any single-family home used only casually by three or four people.

At a certain point, all of the features that began as necessary enhancements to make things more acceptable in a communal home start to reach a level of completeness and quality that begins to capitalize on the enhanced social atmosphere and combined buying power of such a home. We began to see high-performance activity areas that probably made many of you consider such a way of living to be even a bit better than a private life <u>alone</u> in a house with only the most austere features. Efficiencies and environmental benefits started to become more pronounced to the point that some people may not think of living otherwise. Communal living is definitely a way to systematically achieve what we need, while disconnecting ourselves from the lottery mentality of foolishly thinking we can simply win our way to a better life.

Although homes are a fundamental part of everyone's life, few people actually realize how much performance can be built into them. Residents of an MRH would enjoy a **30% increase in free time** throughout their working lives due to:

- Far greater efficiency that requires only a 32-hour workweek
- The mutual support of others who handle the basic chores
- The ability to work at home, which avoids about five hours of travel a week

This additional free time literally amounts to another **13 years** of free time added to our private lives over the span of a typical 45-year working career—definitely something to strongly consider, given the high-performance recreation facilities that are available to enjoy!

To fully demonstrate these possibilities, this chapter will feature five conceptual MRH facilities that will range in size from seven to 21 levels, offering an unprecedented 88% to **98%** reduction in land usage despite a vastly improved quality of living! Achieving both, largely thought impossible, is the benefit of taller multistory buildings and the inherent efficiency of organized communal living.

Are you prepared to live <u>more</u> fully?

Thoughts on Community Support

It's important to realize that larger buildings can have great potential benefit to their community during a crisis. Residents can offer the use of the home's belowground parking facilities to police, medical, and other such services during the intense recovery operations in the aftermath of a disaster. This is important, especially when we see how such services literally flood into an area to help in its recovery. Such protective garage bays would be able to house National Guard trucks with their precious loads of fuel, food, and medical supplies in situations where few other buildings are left standing. Residents can offer the extensive visitor accommodations of the home to displaced citizens and relief workers. Emergency rainwater storage tanks—fueled by the storms themselves—enable a great number of people to continue to bathe, drink, and cook. Backup well water shafts would supplement city and rainwater supplies. Ground-level bathroom and shower facilities, intended to support large outdoor get-togethers at the home, can similarly be opened for public use.

Adding such a hint of emergency support abilities to these homes, at very little cost to residents, helps to prevent a humanitarian downslide from cascading to a point of no return. All it takes is an understanding that the home may need to function in this role someday. Then, as we add the features that residents would need regardless, they are added with this additional *emergency twist* in the way in which they can be used.

The Cornerstone 42-Bedroom/7- to 8-Level Service and Living Center

This is the first true multi-residential home design we have come to. It is the size of a small office building and will actually serve many of the same functions. The building **(Figures 29 to 35)** is 99.4 x 99.7 (30.3 x 30.45 m) and will contain over 69,450 square feet overall: 57% more volume than the last six-level home discussed in Chapter 4. The home has a footprint of 9,927 square feet (923 m²) (about the land area of two tennis courts) and a maximum capacity for 84 main residents and up to 24 visitors. This residential capacity allows for about 20 at-home workers. There will be two freight-size elevators, well-insulated two-foot-thick exterior walls, and an earthquake-resistant foundation.

This facility will have substantial self-supporting home-based businesses. Several private practices, such as a dentist, an optometrist, and a chiropractor, could form the core businesses, while craft, woodworking, sewing, and a small automotive shop would enable residents to provide most other services for themselves. Adding to this heightened level of income-generating self-sufficiency, there will be an astounding 70% reduction of external surface area over an equivalent number of individual homes, which improves efficiency and lessens maintenance costs. Environmentally, this home uses about <u>88%</u> less land than 27 individual homes on a community-wide scale. Ten such buildings would replace a sprawling community of 270 homes and 30 to 50 additional businesses!

Within the home's 15 office-styled bathrooms, there are 42 toilet stalls, 12 urinals, 35 sinks, 13 showers, 4 tubs, and 6 janitorial/bathroom supply stations. Upgraded features in this home include a fully accessible customer parking garage, an animal clinic/kennel, a rooftop courtyard/volleyball court, an extra high parking garage, and side-by-side elevators.

This is the oldest home design presented in this book. It's included here because it demonstrates what features are possible in a design of this size, and was always one of my favorite/heartfelt designs! Potential concerns are its *shared* office-styled bathrooms and its smaller bedrooms. Compared to the 11.1 x 17.7 master bedroom suites that are featured in my other homes, the smaller 8.5 x 13.8 **cabin-style** bedrooms of this design had fairly limited internal storage and somewhat limited access to the bed. Instead, it uses flexible hallway storage and relies on yacht-like interior design to make the smaller bedrooms more acceptable.

The cabin bedroom's 8.5-foot width is deliberately made narrow to encapsulate a king-sized bed on three sides at one end of the room with 12-inch padded armrests and a headboard. Armrests would have cup holders, directional lights, and so on. To access the bed, people would enter at the base and *scoot up* to their respective sides—a relatively small price to pay for a bedroom that saves space while offering more functional armrests than a typical nightstand arrangement. If these smaller bedrooms are not acceptable, this same floor plan could be adjusted to offer nineteen larger bedroom suites with a similar amount of wardrobe space held internally. The two shared bathrooms could also be replaced with four smaller men's and women's bathrooms: still shared, but among the same gender.

Figure 29 – The Basement Level (Customer Parking):

This 12.5-foot-high parking level can hold 13 vehicles of nearly any size. This capacity is proportional to the needs of our six home-based businesses and our after-hour visitor needs **(see Appendix D on page 122).** Anticipating peak visitor parking demands to be during slow customer times allows us to streamline the amount of parking we provide. Each of the six side-bays is 23.3 feet (7.1 m) wide. When used by residents, such a two-car bay width can hold three subcompact cars side-by-side with 1.6 feet (.5 m) of separation, or two eight-foot-wide commercial trucks with 2.3 feet of separation. The top right side-bay can be up to 28.5 feet (8.7 m) deep: deep enough for a 20-passenger shuttle or construction equipment. To facilitate a vehicle's need to turn around when departing, there is a lazy-susan rotating platform (lower center), which can spin a UPS delivery truck right in place. A parking attendant/security guard station is right below this. The 31-foot-wide central access aisle is sized to serve as extra parking space during off-hours. It can hold three vehicles abreast, four deep.

For safety reasons, the home's stairwells are placed in opposite corners. The lower stairwell even has a fire pole shaft running down through the building. The home also has two large elevators (bottom center) that are more efficiently placed side-by-side to save on time and energy. To the right of the elevators is a retail store for our craft businesses or, say, to sell our excess furniture. Having the store on this level keeps elevator usage down. Lower right is a bath/changing room and a stockroom. Above the bathroom is a 10-seat waiting room for visitors, customers, and residents (waiting for a ride).

Below the top right stairwell are a vent shaft and a machinery room for a generator and heating and cooling units. The three stock and storage rooms (found throughout) hold extra bags of cement, wall and flooring material, extra windows, plumbing and electrical supplies, as well as ladders and scaffolding. Driveway salt, bolt-on window shields, and a large air compressor could also be stored here. Under the elevating driveway ramp (that acts like a drawbridge between parking levels) is a place for rainwater holding cisterns, emergency fuel tanks, wellheads, and maintainable sewer, city water, power, and phone hookups, which saves from having to dig up the street to repair a faulty connection.

Figure 30 – Ground Level (Residential Parking):

The 33-foot-wide 17.4-foot-high central parking area is shown with two rows of cars and vans and one row with a 40-foot-long RV and a semi-rig. Along the right outer row of vehicles is a 4.8-foot-wide walkway for people to get to their vehicles or back to the elevators. It also provides access to the indented area down near the elevators, which can hold five motorcycles. Along the left row of vehicles are floor-to-ceiling shelving units for various work-related supplies and bay conversion items.

Center right there is a 40.7-foot-deep side-bay for recreational equipment such as canoe trailers, snowmobiles, and farm equipment that would use the side exit. Such internal accommodations are vital; otherwise, such recreational items end up parked out on the lawn. This side-bay can be closed off from the rest of the garage with an internal roll-down-type garage door, and can also be used for vehicle maintenance. The restoration of an antique car over several months can earn residents tens of thousand of dollars, not to mention how much it could save on automotive repair bills. Below this bay, along the outer wall, is an automotive workbench room, which can be closed off to keep clutter out of sight.

Lower right are two bathrooms on either side of the home's breezeway back exit/trail departure point. Such ideally located bathrooms (which have two showers and three toilet stalls each) can support hikers, bikers, people working out back, or even displaced neighbors in need of basic facilities after a disaster. Directly above this back exit is the home's camping center, which is a place where residents consolidate, organize, and maintain up to 24 mountain bikes and their camping and hiking gear. An exterior lawn and garden closet can be seen on the lower right side. The hallway by the elevators has a phone booth and a place for carts, dollies, wheelchairs, and car care items.

Bottom center is a variable-level scissor-lift truck dock. Tractor-trailer-sized moving vans can back all the way up to this position to offload. Left is a large votech-quality 19 x 47 shop for light manufacturing and there is a shop storage room down in the lower left corner.

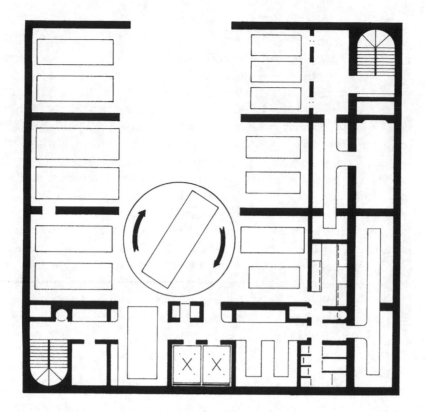

- Figure 29 -

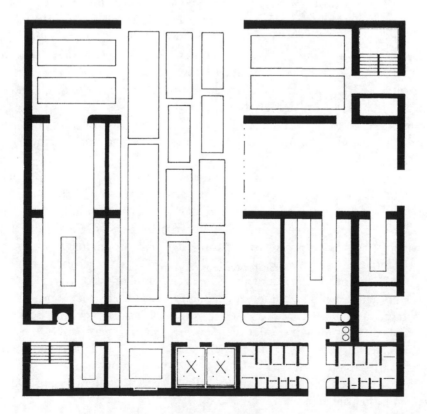

- Figure 30 -

Figure 31 – Level 3 (Partial Kennel Level):

The 5.3-meter-height of the garage below extends up two floors in places. This allows it to be used for such things as warehousing or manufacturing. In these instances, residents would simply park on the customer level, forgo customer-type services, and focus on the production of goods or the storage of bulk supplies. Around the outside of the top part of this central garage area is a partial 7.4-foot-high level that has room for a large 1,800-square-foot animal kennel (bottom right) where pets could be kept comfortably and humanely indoors if several residents were highly allergic to them. Down the right side, the kennel will have six 6 x 6 pens (each with a bay window) for up to 12 dogs. To the right of the elevators is a 12 x 17 (3.6 x 5.3 m) open balcony area where residents can sit out with them. To get pets down to the back exit quickly, pets would be run down a special pull-down ramp (right of the terrace) that can be lowered flush with the floor below. There is also a storeroom for food and supplies to the right of this. Above the pull-down ramp are a room for grooming and bathing and an exam/treatment room for veterinarians to use. Above the balcony there is a section for up to 24 large kitty pens. After owners have visited with their pets, they can use the half bath and a special cleanup station (above the elevators) where they can brush and vacuum off their clothing.

This level also has ample storage space for the work level, and an additional conversion closet, which allows residents to switch between trades and professions without having to sell off trade-related equipment. There will be an additional walk-in freezer, storage for more camping and biking gear, as well as space for toys, yard furniture, and games: eight storerooms in all (left and lower left).

Figure 32 – Level 4 (Work Level):

Working at home is one of the main benefits of communal living. On this level (running right up the center) there are no less than nine 10.3 x 11.3 office/exam/treatment rooms in support of the home's three main health-related businesses and a three-room suite at the top for either a law or designing firm. There are also four 11.3 x 15.4 general trade rooms (immediately above the stairs and bathrooms in the lower left), which round out the home's customer-related businesses. These businesses are supported by a 14-seat waiting room and a reception desk/cashier's station (just right of the elevators). Left of the elevators are two men's and women's bathrooms. One of the three toilet stalls in each is a composting toilet, which has a receptor bin down on the ground level directly below. Above the bathrooms are display cases for our homemade products and the other goods we have for sale. Customer areas are located away from noisier shop and activity areas.

Above the block of four work/trade rooms there are two side-by-side craft rooms, and (in the upper left) a second 23 x 26 sub-industrial-scale shop that has area for bulk storage, an engine lab, and a workbench room. One of the 15.4 x 23 craft rooms will be for group projects and home schooling. The other is intended to support our manufacturing businesses as say an electronics repair lab.

Down the right side we see another equipment/machinery room, a small half bath, a 9.8 x 16.4 eight-seat conference/project room, a bank vault, and a LAN/server computer room (lower right). Left of the server room is the home's main office, where staff members sort mail, pay bills, and schedule appointments. Residents can also use this office during off-hours as a living/work area. Across the hall from the machinery and conference rooms are six 11.3 x 12 project rooms that are provided for residents with a hobby. Two or three residents can use them simultaneously.

Such services, practices, and manufacturing abilities found on this level not only benefit residents and earn money from customers, they also create a level of self-sufficiency that becomes more vital the worse things get. Eye, dental, and other such general care services can provide basic care for a small community in emergencies and to residents to help lower their health insurance costs. Such work facilities (with a staff right on site) may even receive government grants as a way to lessen travel on ultra congested highways or to lessen the vulnerability of manufacturing centers by spreading them out away from the concentrated industrial areas.

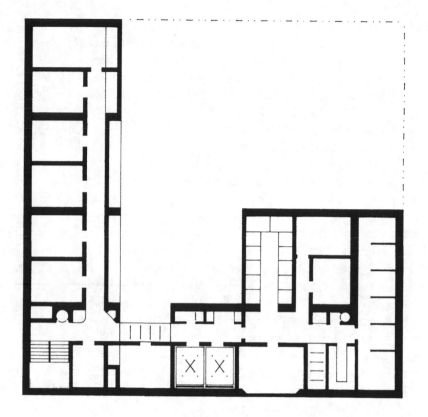

- *Figure 31 -*

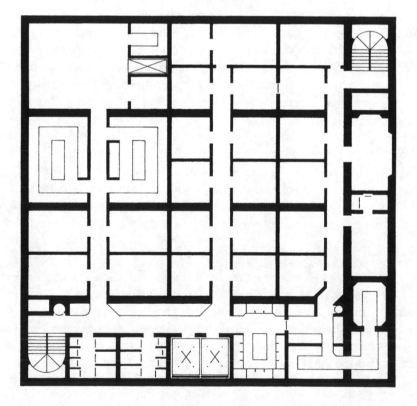

- *Figure 32 -*

Figure 33 – Level 5 (Recreation):

Upper left are two 13 x 21 and 12 x 13 music rooms and an adjoining recording room. Music rooms are located away from most other areas. The smaller music room could become a card table room, too. Top center is a 21 x 23.2 (6.4 x 7.1 m) pool table game room. Upper right is a 17 x 23.2 32-seat state-of-the-art movie theater/conference room. The hallway used to access the theater is flanked by a movie and music library for some 1,500 VHS movies and 2,190 CDs as well as a table and shelves to support all of the various activities in this versatile room. The hallway running horizontally under the theater also serves as a walk-through library for some 6,203 one-inch-thick volumes. Below the music rooms is an 18.7 x 23.2 yoga and martial arts training room (sized for eight to twelve practitioners) and a 14 x 23.2 exercise/weight room (with shelving for accessories and a TV/VCR). The music, game, and exercise rooms are all huddled around an 8.5 x 23 conversion closet (XX) where extra musical instruments, exercise equipment, and alternate games are kept. This closet also provides a sound buffer between rooms. Just outside of the game and exercise rooms (to the left) are two eight-person seating booths or micro-living rooms (which take the room out of the room) and two phone booths.

Below the exercise area is a block of five rooms. Clockwise from upper left there is an 11.3 x 14.8 conference/training room, two boys' and girls' playrooms, an elderly living room (ideally located by the bathrooms, kitchen, and elevators), and an eight-station 11.3 x 24 PC research den/classroom (above the lower stairs). To the right of the lower stairwell is a 21-seat 11.4 x 25.6 dining room with nine outward facing window seats and three four-person dining booths. Above the dining room are snack and beverage counters and a buffet for serving meals. Untimely phone calls can be taken in the extra-wide phone booth (above the right elevator). Since your kids would have a phone too, you could call them internally to tell them to get their asses to dinner. No surcharges would be applied even if there were a *"YES Sir"* or *"YES Mam"* reply from the other end!

Lower right is the 11 x 23 commercial kitchen (with three-foot-deep countertops) and walk-in refrigerator and freezer units. Along the lower hallway are a pantry area (with three-foot-deep floor-to-ceiling shelves) and an at-home worker hallway workstation (with chair) right outside the kitchen. From here, they can plan meals, track inventory, or take call-in orders from residents. As seen on all levels, there is a Jeffrey's tube access ladder built into the wall of each level right by this hallway workstation.

Since cooking, doing dishes, stocking shelves, and doing laundry are the main responsibilities of the support staff, all of these areas are placed close together. Just above the pantry and kitchen area, for example, are a 10 x 25 laundry/utility room with four commercial washers and dryers, three commercial hot water heaters, ironing boards, and a dry-cleaning press. Above this is a six-stall, two-shower bathroom that has been positioned to support the three 9.8 x 18.4 eight-person visitors' rooms (running down the right side). With two showers, all 24 visitors can shower in 2.5 hours. Such an array of visitors' rooms allow us to support conference room activities as well as to help friends in need. Shelving units along the rightmost corridor are also provided for gear or personal belongings. The 12 x 14 visitors' living room and a general living room (above the bathroom) help keep other areas (used for residents only) more private. Our conference room capacity is proportional to our visitor capacity.

Figure 34 – Levels 6-7 (Sleeping and Storage):

The home's two sleeping levels have twenty cabin-style bedrooms each. Bedrooms (averaging about 8.5 x 13.8) are along the outer walls with bathrooms and bulk storage areas **(67 square feet per bedroom)** in the center. Each of the two bathrooms has four toilet stalls, a shower, tub, three sinks, and a urinal. There is one toilet stall for every 2.5 bedrooms, and one shower for every five bedrooms. The average travel distance from the bedrooms to one of these bathrooms is 24 feet. On each floor (in the center and along the corridors) there is over 370 feet of closet storage length. This is enough to provide <u>each</u> bedroom with 19 feet (5.8 m) of external storage on top of the six additional feet of storage found within each room. Amazingly in this design, only four of forty bedrooms sit between two other bedrooms. Hallways on this level, and indeed throughout the home, are 4.6 feet (1.4 m) wide.

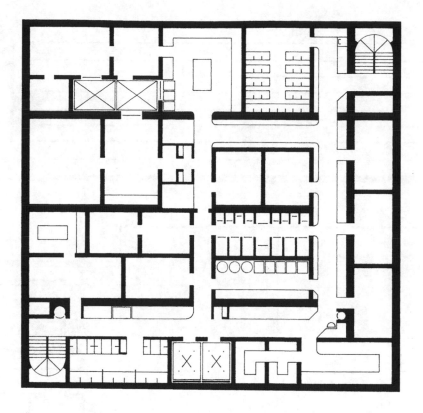

- Figure 33 -

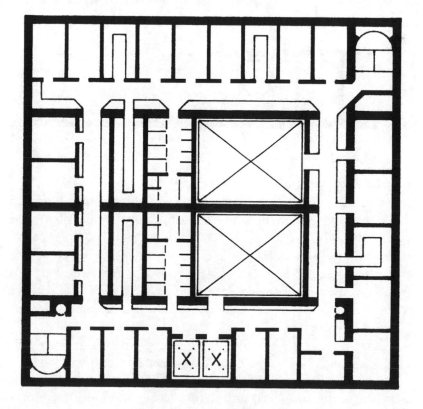

- Figure 34 -

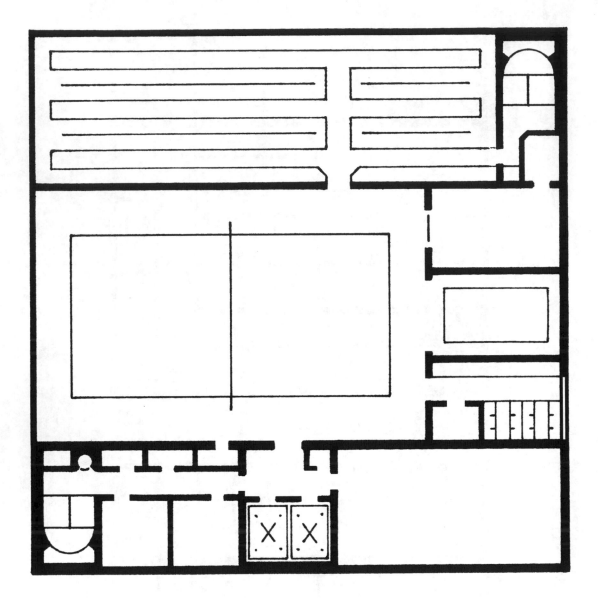

Figure 35 – Level 8 (Add-on Rooftop Activity Level):
　　The amazing features found on this level can be added over time depending on the financial situation of the home's residents. Running across the center is a regulation volleyball court that can also be used to play half-court basketball. Center right is an equipment/machinery room, a Skycar/Airbike hangar, and a 12-seat terrace seating area with beverage counter and an accessories closet. Across the top is a greenhouse that is able to provide every resident of the home with **71 square feet** of vegetable growing area. Lower left are two 12.3 x 12.3 bedrooms, two half baths (one accessed from courtside), and a separate shower room. Lower right is a racquetball court with a phone booth out by the elevators.

　　The smallest home able to offer similar rooftop and garage features would have a footprint of about 800 m². A slightly larger 27.2 x 37.8 m design could offer lower land use and cost (thanks to having three sleeping levels with 13 full-size bedrooms (with double-door side-entryways) and eight cabin bedrooms for teens per level) and a full 16 x 37 m rooftop tennis/basketball court running end to end. Such a design would require the greenhouses be moved to over the flow-by driveway and a separate 'stacked' automated parking garage for customers.

Figure 36: This photo is of an existing six-level building and is shown here just to give you an idea of the size of building we are talking about. With only six (aboveground) levels, it would fit well into most small communities or even out along a country road where saving land is even more important.

How Land Use is Calculated:
Ten Factors to Consider on a Community-Wide Scale

1). At 80% capacity (with 67.2 residents) this last 42-bedroom home would be the equivalent of 26.9 separate single-family homes with an average of 2.5 residents each. 26.9 homes (like my mother's townhouse) would use 3,846 m² of **land,** not counting the lot.

2). 26.9 **driveways** like my mom's (which uses 46.3 m² of land) would total 1,245.5 m². The Cornerstone multi-residential home has a two-lane 7.4 x 30 m driveway and would use only 222 m² of land. Juniper gardens planted on top of driveway overhangs can further reduce our *effective* land use.

3). Individual homes require **roads** to access them. 26.9 homes, with a 23 m wide front yard each, would need a total of 2,412.9 m² of roadway (counting half of a 7.8 m wide two-lane road). Cornerstone itself is only 30.3 meters wide. If it were situated on a 90 m wide property, it would only need 351 m² of road and save 2,061.9 m² of otherwise wasted land.

4-5). Consider how Cornerstone saves 922 m² of land because of its eight **at-home businesses** that are not needed elsewhere. Additionally, these eight home-based businesses are supported by 13 **customer parking spaces,** which at 2.8 x 9.6 m (counting half the access aisle) would typically use up 349.4 m² of land in the form of a one-level parking lot.

6-7). The eight businesses that this home replaced would have additionally needed **driveways** and **roadways** to access them. If one-third of these businesses (2.6) had a 30-meter driveway, they would have needed 577.2 m² more land. If the other two-thirds (5.3) had a 25-meter-wide property, they would have needed 516.8 m² of more asphalt.

8). If the 50 adults working at home had to travel out to eight places of employment instead, they would have needed 50 **employee parking spaces,** which would consume 1,344 m² of land. Cornerstone's lower-level garage doesn't consume any additional land.

9). Cornerstone has 555 m² of **hydroponics growing area** on its rooftop level. Growing vegetables indoors can double the length of the growing season, thus, producing as many fresh vegetables as that typically grown on 1,110 m² of temperamental farmland.

10). When Cornerstone's fully featured **rooftop facilities** are completed, its rooftop volleyball and racquetball courts would save 406 m² of land that would have otherwise been used at a local gym or park for these activities.

All totaled, 26.9 individual single-family homes, roads, driveways, businesses, farming fields and recreational areas would have used 12,729.8 m² of land. Cornerstone itself would use only 1,495.6 m² of land. **That's __88.3%__ LESS LAND!**

The "Warhorse" Nine-Level/81-Bedroom
Service and Living Center

This next design helps to firmly demonstrate the potential value of communal living by offering nearly every benefit that is possible in such homes. It is also one of the smallest designs capable of having a full rooftop basketball/tennis court. It is 130 x 135, contains 157,200 square feet (sf) overall, and has a maximum capacity of 162 residents and 96 visitors. This capacity allows a staff of about 42 at-home workers who are available to support the income-generating efforts of other residents. There would be:

6 Cooks	1 Mechanic	4 Office Workers	3 Shoppers
3 Teachers	1 Superintendent	2 Shuttle Drivers	4 Laundry
3 Nurse/Daycare	3 Hydroponics Gardeners	6 Flex-Workers	6 Security

With 5,000 sf of shop space, 2,800 sf of office space, 1,900 sf of retail stores, 1,756 sf of workroom area, 1,317 sf of project area, 1,280 sf of craft area, an 832 sf automotive garage, and up to 11 work-related vehicles (including semi-rigs and a backhoe), **all** residents can work productively right from this facility! These figures do not even include reception desks, waiting rooms, shop storage, or other such support features. There is a 200-line commercial phone system, an interlinked server computer system, and a parking capacity for dozens of vehicles.

At 80% capacity, the home would have 129.6 residents and would use **92.4**% less land than an equivalent number of 51.8 separate homes (with an average of 2.5 residents each) and various businesses (on a community-wide scale). Even when compared with the 23-bedroom, multifamily home offered up front, this home would use 40% less land.

The home would be constructed of exotic new steels and concrete **(Figure 37)** that don't rot out over time like wood, and a shock-resistant foundation enabling this building to last far longer and withstand greater natural disasters along the way. Structural walls are 20 inches thick and can be seen consistently on every level. Emergency fuel and large rainwater holding tanks would make use of the area under the home's driveway. They help protect against shortages, droughts, and water contamination, which are common after natural disasters. Separate plumbing systems within the home for gray-water (from showers and sinks) and wastewater could make much of the water used in the home easier to treat and even reused for certain things like flushing the toilets and watering the gardens.

Figure 37: Advanced concrete that is **10 times** stronger than today's industrial strength concrete which can actually be seen bending. Photo courtesy of the Surendra P. Shah (ACBM Center Director).

Figure 38 – The Basement Level (Customer Parking):

This 12.5-foot-high basement parking level can hold 15 customer minivans in five 20 x 30 side-bays. The sixth 29 x 30 side-bay (upper right) holds things like the home's 22-passenger shuttle van and other backhoe-sized construction equipment. Bottom right is an automotive service garage complete with hydraulic lift. To the left of this are an engine dismantlement area, a half bath, and an office. The automotive garage may also feature an in-floor-servicing pit to allow access to all of the brakes, suspension, and drive linkage shafts of a large multi-wheeled vehicle.

Right are two 24.3 x 35.4 Votech-quality wood and metal shops that are divided by separate storage and assembly areas. Such shops give this home light manufacturing abilities as well as extensive areas for hobbies. Residents could manufacture things like canoes, custom-made furniture and knives, and even racing engines from scratch. Inward of these shops is a 70-foot-long workbench room that supports shop, automotive, work vehicle, and home maintenance activities.

Left are several retail stores and a central stockroom. Lower left is another store, as well as a 12-seat waiting room, a reception/guard station (with rapid access ladder and fire pole shafts leading to the two floors above), two half baths, and the home's three elevators. On average, one of these elevators will be just one floor away when called for. The hallways (and each of the three widely separated corner stairwells) are all 4.9 feet wide. There are also four corner ventilation shafts.

To cut down on the amount of driveway space needed for a down-ramp, there is a single, elevating-driveway ramp (servicing both parking levels), like those found aboard vehicle ferries. Just outside of the garage entrance there is also a rotating lazy-suzan platform large enough to pin a charter coach right in place.

Figure 39 – Ground Level (Residential Parking):

The 33.8-foot-wide center section of this parking level (which extends up two floors in some sections) is seen with six subcompact cars, five minivans, a 45-foot charter coach (alternating with the home's RV), and two semi-rigs. Five of the side-bays are shown holding six more minivans, three pickup trucks, two ambulance-size work trucks, and 12 motorcycles (--). Side-bays containing work-related vehicles have extensive 30-inch-deep floor-to-ceiling shelving units. This allows carpenters and electricians to restock their vehicles as needed. Four of these side-bays are 20 feet high and can hold additional vehicles stacked on elevating deck plates. Significant rafters exist above other areas for recreational items, tractor accessories, and even cars.

Left are eight street-level 10.8 x 16.4 offices. As storefronts, such sizable rooms can also serve as a hair salon, a florist, a sub shop, an electronics lab, or a used furniture store. Lining the left-hand hallway are storage cabinets/product display cases and eight bench seats. Lower left are a reception desk/cashier, two phone booths, and highly accessible men's and women's bathrooms (with three toilet stalls and one shower unit each). Lining this area are various storage cabinets intended for car care and driveway support items, as well as a place to store carts, dollies, a wheelchair, or any passenger seats temporarily removed from a minivan.

Bottom center is a variable-level, scissor-lift truck dock (which retracts to be flush with the bay floor and can extend up to the height of the rafters). To the right of this dock is a temporary storage space for supplies and furniture being off loaded and a two-station bicycle maintenance shop that serves as a ready-up and trail departure point. Twenty-five MTBs (as well as kids' toys) are stored inward of the bike shop, where there is also a small office for our vehicle-based businesses. Lower right is an exterior agricultural tractor shed, two music rooms, and a punching bag room that is located well away from other areas. Upper right is another large sub-industrial-scale shop.

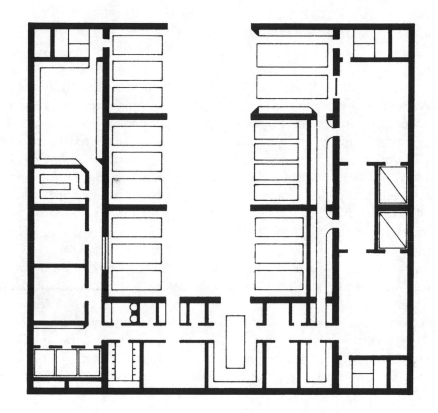

- Figure 38 -

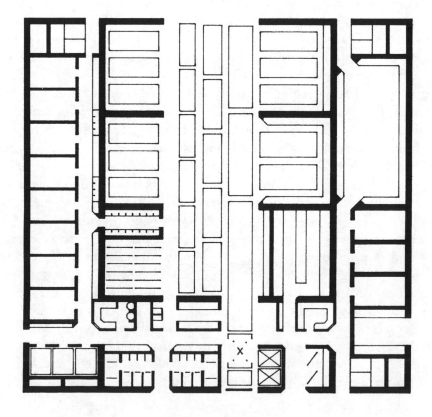

- Figure 39 -

96

Figure 40 – Level 4 (Work/Activity Level):

Level 3 (which exists only around the outside of the 20-foot-high central parking area) isn't shown. It would have shops, customer offices, and an animal kennel/clinic. Level 4 (shown here) has a combination of features. Upper middle holds an 84-seat movie theater/conference center (which can potentially earn the home as much as $52,000 during a one-week conference), a smaller 38-seat theater/conference room, a bank vault, computer room, and a home office. Lower middle is the home's 20-person 30 x 36 martial arts/yoga training area supported by two bathrooms, two locker rooms, and a conversion closet. This training area could potentially earn $600 a day or almost $150,000 a year in class dues! The strategically placed conversion closet (to the right) allows the training area to serve as a living area, workroom, or as a place for live performances and plays when needed. It also allows equipment in the nearby exercise and game rooms to be swapped out with other pieces of equipment and games periodically.

Bottom center are three 11 x 21.3 trade-related workrooms, a support closet, and the home's two-pool table game room/sports bar (with seating for 18). Top center are ten project rooms for hobbies and crafts (like painting, sculpture, and bow making), a meeting/training room, a supply closet, and a half bath. Right are three 18.7 x 23 craft rooms (overflowing with durable, damage-resistant workbenches and storage cabinets) for group activities and home schooling. There is also a similarly sized exercise/weight room, another storage closet, and two more bathrooms on this side. Lower left (by the elevators) is a waiting room and reception desk for customers. Upper and middle left are five more workrooms and a conference center support room (center left) with four phone booths, eight-computer workstations, a closet, and a seating booth.

Figure 41 – Level 5 (Living and Visitors Level):

The middle section of this level contains twelve 10.1 x 17.7 eight-person bunk bedrooms for up to 96 visitors. For privacy, the top half of each bunk is enclosed by a floor-to-ceiling nightstand (which also serves as the ladder to the top bunk and as a nightstand on the inside). The base of each bunk is also enclosed. Supporting visitors and conference attendees are two main men's and women's bathrooms (center) and a visitors' support room with phone booths and computer workstations (center left). Twelve highly customized, 11.1 x 18.7 age-oriented living rooms can also be found around the top and left-hand sides of this floor. Such living rooms would be well furbished (styled much like a yacht cabin) to make as much use of this space as possible.

Bottom left is the 48-seat, low-light dining room that is able to seat everyone in the home at a max capacity (258 people) in six dining period rotations from, say, 4:30 to 7:30. A four-period rotation during normal times is much more common. At night, the dining room can transform into a social area or a nightclub on weekends. To the right of the dining area is the commercial kitchen with industrial appliances, a full-blown automated dishwasher, pot-scrubbing sinks, and two walk-in refrigerator/freezer units (each sized for emergency supplies, canning, and wild game meats). The walk-ins are specifically located over the game room below. The six-foot-wide hallway here is lined with a kitchenette and serving counters, three-foot-deep floor-to-ceiling pantry shelves, a janitorial closet, and a damage-control closet complete with ready-to-go fire fighting suits. Amazingly, the amount of square footage used by the kitchen, dining room, pantry, and refrigeration units is 85% lower than what it would be in 51.8 separate homes! In fact, the area of this whole level would have been lost to separate single-family kitchens and dining rooms. Just look at what we gained instead!

Right is one of two hydroponics greenhouses with over 5,200 square feet of growing area. Along the hallway on this side is 700 feet of floor-to-ceiling shelving units for as many as 8,500 one-inch-thick books.

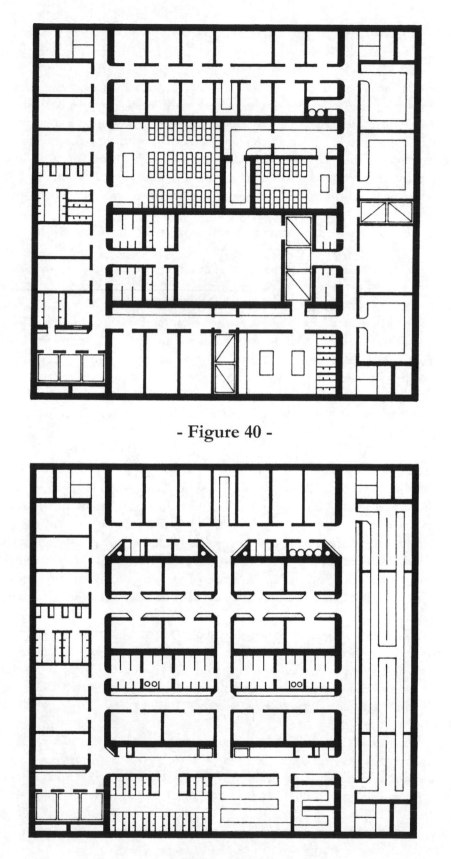

- Figure 40 -

- Figure 41 -

Figure 42 – Levels 6-8 (Sleeping and Storage):

Each of the home's three sleeping levels has 27 11.1 x 18.7 master bedroom suites. They each contain a 12-foot-long desk (located by the windows), and 24.6 feet of hardwood cabinets, shelving, and clothing racks that allow couples to consolidate their belongings. Bedrooms have an allowance for a king-size bed (or side-by-side twin beds) with easy access to both sides, and are wide enough to allow for a small table by the door. Bedrooms are separated by 8-inch-thick walls, do not border a bathroom, and would use high-density exterior-type doors that further reduce noise. Bedroom doorways are at least six feet apart and are not across from one another. Additional wardrobe rooms provide for some additional separation between bedrooms. Kids and infants would share gender-specific rooms and nurseries. Semiprivate rooms would provide Level II nursing home care to the elderly when necessary.

The center section has four main men's and women's bathrooms (with two stalls and two showers each) and two of them have laundry facilities. The ratio of toilet stalls and showers per bedroom is high (one stall for every 2.25 bedrooms) and there are enough shower/tub units to allow everyone on this level to shower within a 1.6-hour timeframe. Surrounding the bathrooms are five large bulk storage rooms, providing every bedroom with **96 square feet** of bulk storage capacity. Lower center is a 30 x 30 great room/living area for residents to relax and unwind in.

Along the inside of the upper and lower hallways are four half baths (to help lower nightly walking distances), two kitchenettes, a small office (for a printer and supplies), janitorial closets, and two phone booths (by the elevators). Upper right are four fire pole shafts: two travel down one floor at a time (one arriving from above and the other going down), while the others travel down two floors at a time (with some floors being bypassed). These shafts help most residents get to the home's lower floors much more quickly.

Figure 43 – Level 9 (Rooftop):

Center is the home's 72 x 120 court/activity area. Horizontal brackets denote the potential for three side-by-side volleyball courts. Vertical brackets show the length and width of a regulation NBA basketball court and a standard tennis court. This area is ideal for parties, summer outings, concerts, nightly stargazing, outdoor Tai Chi, and roller blade hockey. A sizable UH-60 Blackhawk helicopter could actually land within the circular area in the middle, too! The surface of this landing/courtyard-like area could potentially be made of glass or a hard, clear plastic compound with solar collection panels underneath. The home's 100-foot height raises the landing area well above treetop levels for safety.

Sliding partitions can divide the court into separate court and landing areas. Around three sides of this courtyard are shelving units for concert speakers, video and light bars, bench seats, as well as storage lockers for gymnastic equipment, folding tables and chairs, goals, target hay bales, and other sports-related items. A simple, inflatable fabric cover can allow for year-round activities. Around the corners of the building would be strategically placed water cannons to help fight off any approaching wildfires.

At right, is the home's second southern-facing greenhouse with 6,400 square feet of growing area on three-foot-deep racks stacked four high. In total, the home provides all 162 potential residents with **72 square feet** of growing area (the equivalent of 116,000 square feet of seasonally-dependent farmland). Left are two multiuse aircraft hangar/storage bays for Skycars and things like jungle gyms, a 20 x 40 multiuse racquetball court (flanked by bathrooms and eight-person seating booths), and an 18 x 29.5 rooftop living area (lower left) to enjoy activities in. Machinery and equipment rooms would be located above portions of this level.

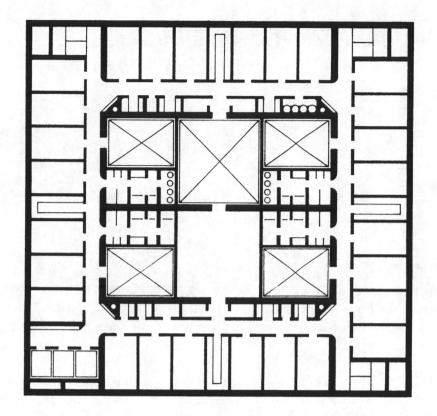

- **Figure 42** -

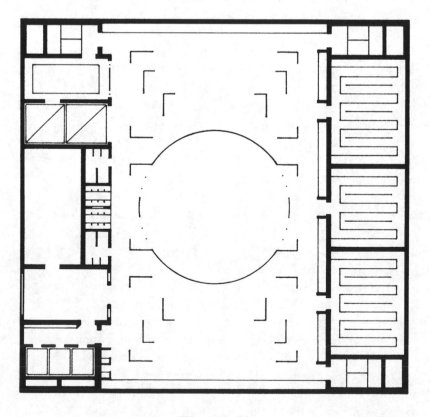

- **Figure 43** -

The Ten-Level/140-Bedroom
Service and Living Center

Large buildings may seem cold or out of place to those unconcerned with land conservation, but they are a panacea for both an improved quality of living as well as far greater efficiency (when they are laid out properly). This next design breaks the mold of what is thought possible. Although only one floor taller than the last design, it has 40% lower land use and its costs per resident are 15% lower. Its octagonal shape is more efficient and offers less wind resistance. With its stairwells, ventilation and elevators shafts, kitchens, and bathrooms placed further inside of the building (within a protective inner core) the building is also able to endure more severe storm damage. Stairwell and elevator access is greatly improved and office, shop, craft, and work areas remain proportional to the number of residents. Overall, such a compact single-building arrangement would be easier to find land for than a sprawling co-housing development.

Although this is a larger building with more residents, individual privacy has been greatly improved over the last design. On each of the five sleeping levels **(Figure 44)** we see 24-master-bedroom suites and four kids' bedrooms (with their own play and study areas) around the outer perimeter. Each is divided from the other by either a three-foot-wide bulk storage closet or an extra thick structural support wall. Two out of every three bedrooms have a more private double-door side entryway and no bedroom borders a stairwell, vent or elevator shaft, or bathroom.

With additional bulk storage rooms in the center, each bedroom has **98 square feet** of individualized bulk storage space available to use. Further increasing privacy is the fact that each sleeping level now has its own living and kitchen areas located in the center of each floor. This prevents residents from having to go down to lower level kitchen or dining facilities that would then have to be shared by residents from all other levels.

Located in the upper center of the drawing are accommodations for 32 visitors, luggage racks, and two bathrooms. Lower center are two more men's and women's bathrooms, a 12-seat dining room, a 12-seat pool table game room, a large kitchen, four phone booths, and a large visitor support room with PC workstations. During dining periods, the 12 seats in the game room can serve as extra dining room accommodations. Inward of the bedrooms are two craft/conference rooms, one exercise room, three large living rooms, and four additional bathrooms. Supplementing these living areas are four small libraries (for up to 4,000 volumes) and four external terraces for up to six people each in the upper and lower corners of the design. A 140-seat movie theater and a large martial arts training gym can also be found on the home's fourth level.

The rooftop level **(Figure 45)** has a similar basketball/tennis/volleyball court area in the center as did the last design, but it has additional recreational areas along the outside. Bottom center are two living areas and a central racquetball court. The lower left- and right-hand corners each have two terraces and a hangar for flying cars. Across the top and down the sides is a massive hydroponics greenhouse, which can provide every resident of the home (at max capacity) with **72 square feet** of 24/7/365 growing area. These greenhouse gardens go from three to eight shelving units high as they slope up to an overall 20-foot height surrounding the central courtyard. In both of the upper two corners of the design is a quiet arboretum area with window seating for 12 people.

This facility is 161 feet in diameter and can support as many as 240 adults, 60 children, and 160 visitors. Each floor has a footprint of 23,216 square feet. The garage levels would have two vehicle elevators and one double-ended garage bay that are similar to the next octagonal design. In an abbreviated form, this design can be used as an emergency center or a series of self-contained defense outposts defending each of our major cities.

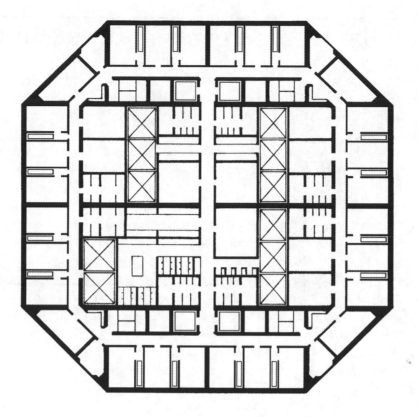

- Figure 44 -

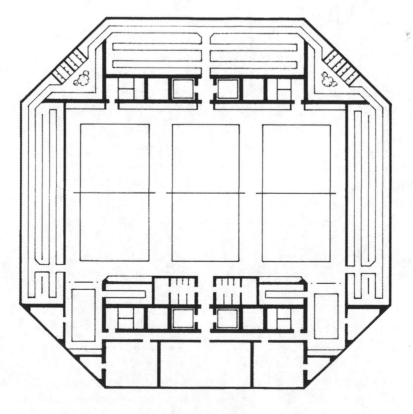

- Figure 45 -

The Combined Emergency/Municipal Center

As we've learned, these larger facilities can serve as enhanced emergency centers in an abbreviated form. These next, much larger 64-meter-diameter designs represent the parking and ground levels of either a 17-level communal facility or a four-level emergency center. As an emergency center (shown), such a facility would combine a community's police, fire, rescue, and health departments as well as provide space for National Guard units and utility services. Such a comprehensive center would be much more functional and better able to support a surrounding community in times of need. In order not to squander this potential, we need to be built them the very best that we can. For any fire or police station or any medical clinic to be just as vulnerable to a natural disaster as the communities they are intended to serve is completely unacceptable!

By employing a battery of lower-level shower and restroom facilities, a cafeteria and commercial kitchen, and segmented eight-person bunk bed rooms, this facility could remain a focal point during the most intense phases of a recovery operation. These bunk accommodations are better than placing cots in an ill-equipped school gymnasium and can accommodate recovery teams and displaced families. There would be emergency generators and fuel supplies for vehicles, a truck loading dock to handle the heavy influx of supplies, and rainwater holding tanks. Wells would be drilled as a backup to public water sources and an independent septic system would be in place in case the main facility was flooded out. Lastly, a flat rooftop would serve as a landing area for police, medical, and relief helicopters sent into an area with supplies and additional personnel.

In **Figure 46** (an underground parking level), we see two separate 20-vehicle garage bays (top and bottom center). An entire police department could be securely housed in just one of these garages. These garages are served by a pair of large vehicle elevators in the upper and lower left, which take up 80% less volume than a down ramp. In the middle and along the sides is a wealth of large storerooms, offices, shops, and waiting areas. Four widely separated stairwells, two groups of four elevators, and four-ventilation shafts can be found within the two areas just inward of the outer hallways on both sides. They are contained within a protective curtain called an ***inner core***. Amazingly, this wind-resistant, octagonal shape would have <u>65</u>% less outer wall length exposed to the elements than that found in six 60 X 120 firehouses of an equivalent volume!

In **Figure 47** (ground level), we see two main 210-foot-long vehicle bays (center right) which can hold four 45-foot ladder trucks, six 30-foot fire engines, two semi-rigs, and up to six ambulances with ample separation. With the left side of the building facing the center of an intersection, these long, flow through-type vehicle bays would form a diagonal link between intersecting roadways. A two-lane back road could even pass right through the building in some cases.

Along the sides of the vehicle bays and hallways are 32-inch-deep floor-to-ceiling shelving units for an untold amount of emergency supplies and apparatus. Trash dumpsters hold position between the vehicle elevators where they are easily accessed. Center left are two long storage rooms and two areas earmarked for the storage of things like police motorcycles, snowmobiles, jet skis, and vehicle attachments (|). There is also a 14-seat high-alert waiting lounge, a service shop for all the various motorcycles, and two bulk storage areas large enough to contain a semi-trailer's entire load. On the rooftop above this center section is a 120 x 210 rooftop landing area. This area is also the same size required for three side-by-side basketball courts or an indoor soccer venue.

The side sections of this level contain four widely separated exits (complete with security checkpoints), storerooms, ration distribution areas, and two large bathrooms (left and right center, accessed from within or without). In all, these bathrooms have a total of 16-toilet stalls, 16-showers, 22 sinks, and four urinals and are a blessing to displaced crowds.

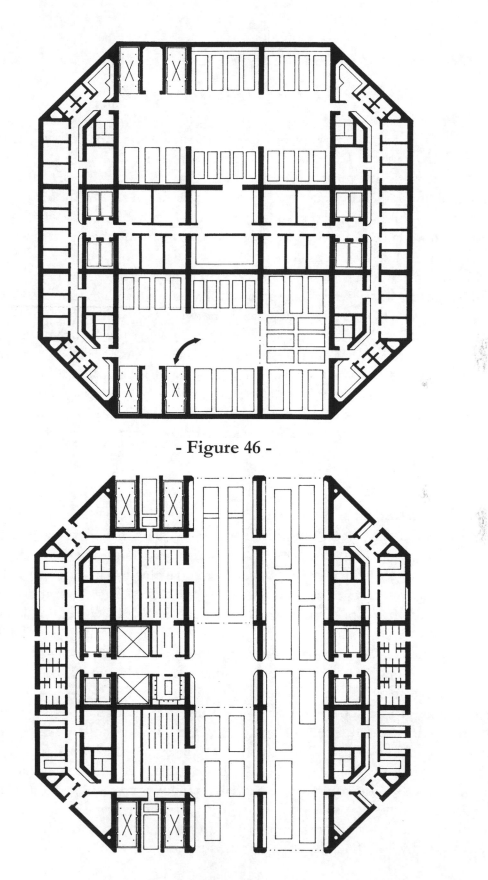

- Figure 46 -

- Figure 47 -

Capstone: A Monolithic Communal/Municipal Mid-Rise Facility

The seriousness of our environmental and humanitarian situation is rather extreme.[21] It will take more than just a few highly efficient communal homes to help slow and reverse this trend. In fact, it will take some 15,000 to 25,000 multi-residential buildings like the last few we saw to house just 1% of the U.S. population. Looking at this number, it becomes clear that still larger, more efficient buildings will be needed in the long run. Although a slow progression from smaller homes to even bigger facilities is the most likely course of action, I had to ask if there wasn't a shortcut. Could we start with larger and more efficient second or third generation facilities first?

We all go through life standing in awe of what ultimately became possible from very meager beginnings. There is the stark contrast between the Boeing 747 and the 1903 Wright Flyer, for example, or the unbelievable difference between the Saturn V moon rocket and the original German V2. Would the same thing eventually apply to communal homes? What is possible? Obviously, there isn't much we can't build when we want to. Believing that I at least needed to see what could be accomplished in a truly massive unit, I set out designing this next 21-level facility without any restrictions in size or cost. All my life I have been fascinated with imposingly large science-fiction ships and self-contained military outposts, which bring what's needed together into a very streamlined and purposeful facility. I wasn't going to turn back now!

Rooftop Facilities:

The initial requirements for this new facility were for it to have rooftop landing facilities able to serve as an ultra-modern transportation hub. There are more than a few examples I can and have given of an upcoming aerial revolution that will help speed local and regional travel through a network of vertaports. Such vertaports would allow helicopter-like aircraft to speed passengers over considerable distances and back: right down to the local level. Even if such a transit revolution is 50 years away, it is still something such a building (designed to last for several thousand years) would need to plan for.

To get passengers to their final destination in any future door-to-door service, secondary landing areas would be needed for smaller flying taxicabs. All of these various landing areas have to be separated from each other (for safety reasons) and separated from the rooftop activity areas that have become so common in my fully utilized rooftop layouts. Large hangars would obviously be needed for both large and small aircraft.

As part of the rooftop layout, I also wanted to have several basketball courts together because three side-by-side courts could actually be converted into an NHL ice hockey rink, which is also the same size as an indoor soccer or an arena football venue. This ultimate new multiuse rooftop activity center would be enclosed on all sides like a courtyard and could be covered by an inflatable fabric roof to support year-round activities.

---

[21] Discovery News reported a potential 30% to 50% mass extinction in the next 100 years!

All of this may sound pretty far-fetched until you actually see just how feasible and indeed how well it all fit together! The actual design is as compact, as versatile, and as functional as any I've created. Think of it as a dream if you must. But, seeing it on paper allows us to gauge for ourselves how inevitable it really is. Remember, the process of analytical design directs us in what to do based on the problems at hand. It is not about just trying to get by or simply hoping for the best.

Ground-level Features:

As with all of my designs, the inside layout of each level has to conform around a set, given arrangement of structural support walls that run from the basement to the rooftop. Instead of evenly spaced pillars, these support walls help to divide each level and, therefore, have to be developed in such a way as to allow each level the spacing it needs. This is obviously a laborious planning nightmare to be sure. Much like the rooftop, the garage and sleeping levels require specific layouts that aren't as flexible in their size or in their shape as the kitchen, living, and work areas found on other levels. Thus, developing the design of these three levels first is of paramount importance. Fortunately, in these last three octagonal facilities, these same structural walls are used to form an *inner-core:* a survivable inner section that protects key areas at the heart of the building from extreme damage.

After allowing the rooftop facilities to grow as much as they needed to, I began to see other potentials in the rest of the design. For example, the building was now large enough to be able to sit directly over a two-lane roadway in order to save as much land as humanly possible. Roads devastate the environment by consuming just as much land as our homes and shopping malls do. Building over them, to make use of this already used land, is a landmark change that finally makes my design goal of achieving a 98% reduction in land use entirely possible! Such a unique arrangement eliminates the wastefulness of expansive driveways and also provided perfect access to the up and down ramps that lead to the four other parking levels that the home is also built over.

Because of the building's sheer size, the most important features of the ground level became its large shipping and receiving truck bays and its extensive bus and taxi transit facilities. There will be so many supplies and so many people on the move on this ground level that such facilities had to be very large, easily accessed by both people and by overly large and awkward vehicles, and yet somehow prevented from interfering with one another. As you will see, these amazing features were blended together and maximized for the first time with little extra land needed to accomplish this.

Living, Work, and Community Support Features:

A facility of this size obviously needs a substantial number of high-quality living and recreational areas. This home is, indeed, built to save land and be as efficient as possible, but no one—including myself—would live in it, if it did not increase our quality-of-living in the process! Fortunately, the tremendous features found on the rooftop and ground levels only hint at what is possible on the building's recreational levels. There will be a 400-person auditorium/IMAX amphitheater as well as several smaller 100-seat theaters. There will be an indoor swimming pool, a half dozen racquetball courts, and so on. This home fights to extend our free time and enhance our full enjoyment of life as much as it attempts to save the environment. Communal living is so efficient that with the right design, both are entirely possible! The design matches the efficiency of a skyscraper in a much smaller facility that is not unthinkable for smaller communities (where their effectiveness can be fully realized). I personally envision them being built in the middle of a forest where they would help preserve the land from the devastating sprawl of a new development!

The home's two work and manufacturing levels give the residents of this facility and those of the surrounding community a substantially higher level of self-sufficiency than any previous design. Such shops would make any number of NASCAR teams green with envy as they can manufacture almost anything they need from scratch. With some 200 living room-sized offices, this building is literally like a focal point of modern services! To help make this facility even more acceptable to a surrounding community, I not only made it into a full-blown transportation hub, I also incorporated many municipality-oriented features and services. On the parking levels, for example, there is room for a fire department and even a police station.

Shape and Cost:

The building's seven-sided, octagon-like shape is best described as having the look of a rough-cut diamond. Overall, it is 103 meters wide and would fill the core of a professional football stadium. It would have 85% less exterior surface area than an equivalent number of single-family homes and businesses.

The facility's $150 million price tag is a lot, but it is actually less than, say, what a Boeing 747 would cost. Such a passenger jet only lasts 25 years, not several thousand, and holds only 400 passengers at a time, not 1,800 residents!

Choosing an Appropriate Name

Much like one does not call a naval vessel or a space station a commune, I do not believe that this label applies to these larger facilities. A commune, to me, represents more of a social movement that is somewhat separate and isolated from what goes on around it. The purpose of these types of buildings is the exact opposite. Much like on a naval vessel, the shared living aspects of these facilities take a backseat to the overriding purpose they embody. Given all of the full-blown manufacturing abilities, services, municipality features, and its public transit abilities, such homes are intended to interact and to provide extensive support to a surrounding community, not withdraw from it!

After thinking about it, the label "The Fully Integrated Service and Living Center" began to sound much more accurate. Integration, for example, means to coordinate and blend into a functioning and united whole. To unite!

As for an actual name for this last design, I chose *Capstone* after the amazing pillars of compressed materials we see out in nature directly below a heavy capstone. The weight of the capstone prevents the material directly below them from being worn away. These natural pillars are often photographed for their striking beauty. I liken this to the way in which this facility would hold the many loose ends of our social fabric together, loose ends that would, otherwise, be washed away to the insanity of the outside world.

The Fully Integrated Service and Living Center

--- Roof --- Communication array / water cannon / solar / defenses / gardens / deck.

19. Partial rooftop upper level – observation areas / 1.5 meter telescope.

18. Main rooftop activity / sports / landing / hangars.

17. Machinery level – gravity feed water tanks / power generation / storage.

16. Hydroponics level / 72 additional bedrooms along outer ring.

15. Storage level / 112 additional bedrooms along outer ring.

14. Adults-only sleeping level / hydroponics in middle.

13. Adults-only sleeping level / hydroponics in middle.

12. Parents' and children's sleeping level / hydroponics in middle.

11. Adults and guests sleeping level / storage in middle.

10. Teen sleeping level / storage in middle.

09. Main recreation, kitchen, and dining level.

08. Children's and infants' care level / storage and kids' rec. in middle.

07. Elderly sleeping level / protected medical center in middle (egress chute).

06. Visitors' sleeping level / additional rec. areas and conference center in middle.

05. Project level / warehouse and vault in the middle (sound buffer over manufacturing).

04. Work / office / shop / lab / manufacturing level.

03. Customer / traveler / employee parking level / extensive retail stores.

02. Customer / traveler / employee parking level / kennel / animal hospital.

-------- GL. Ground level: truck court / pickup points / bus stop / fire department. ---------------

- s1. Residential parking / transit authority / police / vehicle repair garage / farm / underground rail and tunnels / maintainable sewage and water system.

- s2. Visitors / convention parking / indoor 25 and 50 m pools / museum

Figure 48:

This is the home's massive ground-level interface. The home is built over a two-lane country back road (with side parking on the shoulders of the road) and has internal exit ramps (just right of the top and bottom center points) leading to a three-lane bus departure area (with wide side walkways) running parallel with the road. There are two 28-m-deep truck bays (for up to four semi-rigs) and loading docks (with side storage able to hold a tractor-trailer's full load) on the extreme right of the drawing. The truck bays are ideally located so that semis can use the exit ramps as a way to back directly into them. The angle and sizing of these off-and-on exit ramps also makes pulling out into traffic (either way) easier. Extreme left is the semicircle down/up ramps leading to the four other parking levels (for several hundred vehicles). These parking areas will be above and below the roadway and the bus depot in the center of the design. Running down the middle of the drawing (between the roadway and depot) are four customer waiting areas and four large bathroom facilities (top and bottom center). A baggage check and ticket counter is in the exact center.

Figure 49:

This is an example of just one sleeping level. Shown are 180 cabin bedrooms. The 52 separate wardrobe rooms and wardrobe hallways provide an amazing eight meters of closet length per bedroom. In all seven corners of the building there are observation lounges and terraces. There are also four side-by-side male and female bathrooms with 72 stalls and 40 separate showers. The center of the layout is largely used for bulk furniture storage but can hold various movie theaters and recreation areas, too. In the future, such designs will provide larger bedrooms that have their own equivalent of a wardrobe room held in the room itself (as was seen in the 23-bedroom home design mentioned earlier).

Figure 50:

This is the home's fully featured rooftop. Top center is an extremely large courtyard area showing two full NBA basketball courts and a championship-quality tennis court. Jogging lanes around the perimeter of this court area are also available. This entire central area can be converted into an NHL hockey rink, arena football arena, or an indoor soccer venue. Concerts and plays can also be performed here on the large stage just below the bottom most basketball court. This level has two six-place side landing ports (that overhang the sides of the building—left and right center) and a massive main landing area (bottom center—shown with three volleyball courts). The home's two large aircraft hangars (with workstations and side storage) are between the three landing areas and are able to hold a folded V-22 or up to six flying vans. Six waiting rooms flanking the center concert stage can hold as many as 72 residents or passengers waiting to depart. Baggage scanning and control rooms are also present along the landing area's perimeter. There is a gymnastics training hall (upper right) and a full four-room conference center (upper left). At the bottom tip and to the sides of the top basketball court there are three balcony/terrace areas provided for a fantastic view. As shown in all three drawings, the stairs, elevators, bathrooms (for the most part), and ventilation shafts are all in the same areas on each level.

In the distant future, when roads are multilevel, most recreational areas would be above the roadways, providing twice the number of recreation centers per building! Landing areas would still be on the rooftop levels to keep ground-level noise to a minimum.

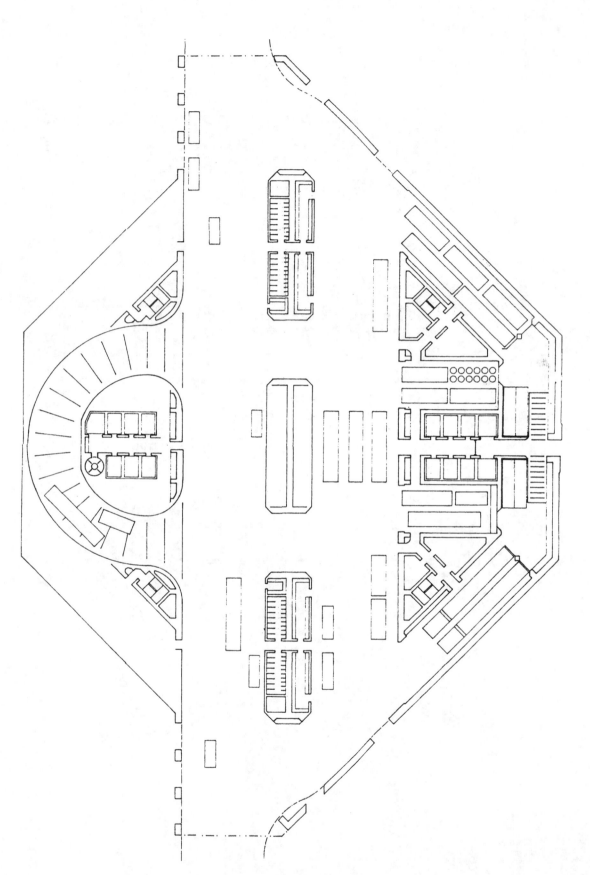

Figure 48

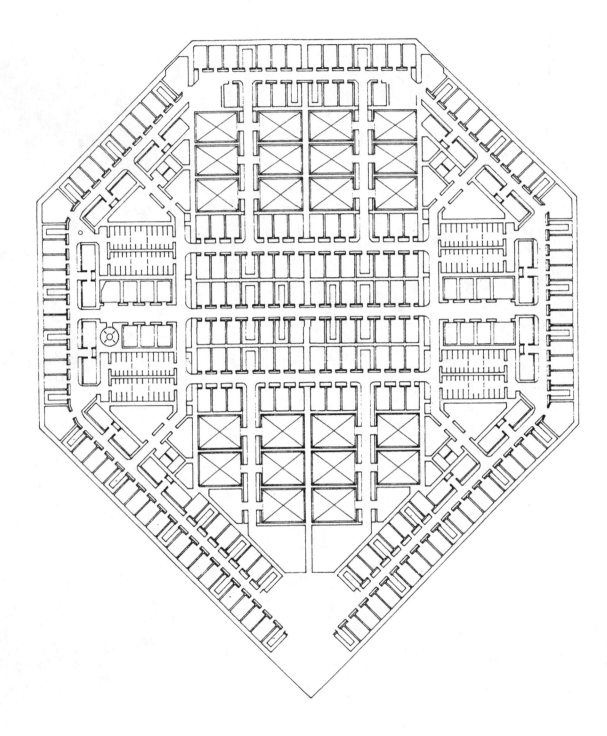

Figure 49

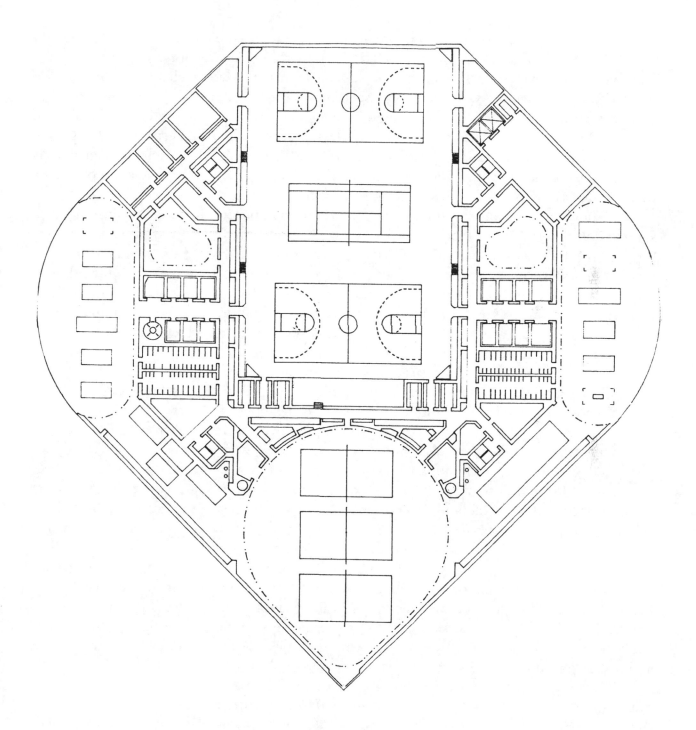

Figure 50

Conclusion

We all have an inherent interest to make the most of our lives and do what we think is right. It is, therefore, critical for us to know what is possible, so that we can determine for ourselves whether it is worth changing our lives for. So much is changing (technologically, socially, and environmentally) that we need to occasionally rethink where it is we should be going and where it might now be possible to get to. Beyond the constraints of cost and ideology, which tend to restrict what a person deems civically or individually possible, we need to determine what is flat-out technically possible. Certainly, anyone would agree that if we had it to do all over again, how much better things could be made the second time through.

The extended-family, multifamily, and the completely featured multi-residential service and living centers that we have seen throughout this book have provided us with very sound and realistic examples of what is technically possible. Such homes will finally make it possible to derive more than just a meager existence from a path laid down by the most carefully placed footsteps of conservation. Only by splicing together all of the tools that we have at our disposal—to function as a single and comprehensive system in a concise and deliberate action of self-enhancement—can we ever hope to achieve an overall balance with nature and a fullness in life.

Though many misgivings exist, communal living is what we make of it. To me, it has always been a way to systematically achieve what we need while disconnecting ourselves from the lottery mentality of foolishly thinking we can simply win our way to a better life. It is not a social statement against Western values. Such values are not wrong. They are just out of proportion. They are used more to portray one's social status than to actually get more out of life. One should not have to work their whole life just to meet the basic essentials of living, but that's about all we are doing when we let slip the home's potential to secure a more comfortable and secure existence for ourselves via the economy of scale of larger and more fully featured facilities. There's just too much to gain when we organize ourselves the best we can, as opposed to a family-by-family/one-for-one haphazard sort of way. The aspect of privacy is too finite and intangible to be given such overriding dominance in the design of something as critically important as the homes we live in. Proper design techniques and high technology can be employed to make adjustments for this essential need, while—at the same time—incorporating so much more that we also would really want in a home, too. Communal living is simply the most natural, efficient, secure, and downright fun way to live when it is done <u>correctly</u>!

In order to gain all the important advantages that communal living has to offer, we must strive to create the most ***functional/high-performance*** home designs we can. Aesthetics and the façade of using showcase-like formal areas must give way to provide adequate habitability. Attempting to get more out of life by using greatly enhanced work and recreational areas must also attempt to do so without simply resorting to the use of more land in the process. These are very stringent and even conflicting design challenges to be sure. However, as we have seen, with the right high-performance multilevel designs, overcoming both of these challenges is entirely possible.

Harmonizing ourselves with the cycles of our planet is indeed a difficult discipline. In many respects our technology offers us the chance to not only coexist with our planet's ecology, but to flourish into something of a proprietary species capable of transcending the greatest gaps of time. There is a noticeable and growing disparity, however, between what is possible with high technology and our society's ability to continuously incorporate its advancements. As the complexity of society has grown, for example, it has become increasingly harder for it to change in all but the subtlest ways. This growing complexity has forced society to spend more and more of its resources on activities needed just to keep itself running, and less on the refinement and implementation of new technology. If we are not extremely vigilant, these two expenditures can and will reach a point of divergence in which we can no longer afford the technology that is needed to continually substitute for the resources we've used up. As promises of being able to power ourselves on the hydrogen from seawater (used in nuclear fusion) slip to a point at least three decades away, it is also becoming apparent that we can no longer afford to wait for it.

If we must cautiously remove whichever hopes we have of receiving a quick fix from such futuristic technology or from some half-baked, pork-ladened government initiative, we are left to essentially draw a circle around ourselves and say, ***"Any solutions are going to have to come from us!"*** Those who step into the circle must somehow accomplish enough good to counter the wrongs of those working only for their own self-interests. Such a historic drive must aim to capture the heart of our <u>full</u> potential so that it lies beyond the reproach of those who might suffer from our inaction. It must also discover how to fundamentally reweave the fabric of society so that it becomes free from the knotted imperfections of waste and the needless overlaps of duplicated effort **(See Appendix I on page 132).** This is something that I truly believe communal living is all about. Faced with having to establish a path that will lay unbroken by doubts that more could have been done, where else do we turn?

Rather than trying to display our wealth with fancy, impractical homes that get us nowhere, people need to stand shoulder-to-shoulder in the protection of their families and the environment! Communal home designs are, in this sense,

"The very last lines in the sand left to draw!"

Note: As a communal living activist, I am hoping to begin just such a community based on these multistory, ultra land-conscious designs. My listing **(The Deliberacy...)** can be found in the printed and online versions of the **2007 Communities Directory:** http://directory.ic.org. See you there!

Appendix A:
Common House Problems

Although outwardly there seems to be many reasons for a central common house, its main feature—an expensive, restaurant-sized kitchen and dining area—basically only duplicates the kitchen and dining areas present in each individual home of the development. It's like trying to argue that every housing development needs its own restaurant, which is horrifically wasteful—even more so than current society is. The presence of all these other individual kitchens markedly dilutes the whole intended purpose for having such a high-performance restaurant. To my total dismay, the commercial-quality kitchen facilities of one community's common house were only serving three dinners a week and did not offer breakfast or lunch.

Although another community of 90 people I visited served dinner every day (and lunches on occasion) in their common house, I noted that 95% of the time fewer than six people could be found in this massive building, most of whom were just passing through or talking. This was also because of the existence of so many other kitchens and recreation areas in the community's other widely separated buildings. Even well planned and interesting activities had poor attendance. Another problem I noted was that the kitchen staff was constantly rotated, which led to substantially reduced efficiency.

To me, common houses are extremely wasteful, regardless of any "eco-friendly" claims a community might have. The two I have seen in person were sprawling one- and two-level buildings that wasted land. The floor plans I've seen for others were even more wasteful. All of these common houses had a fancy exterior finish and a large cathedral ceiling. To me, this is just wasted space that you don't even notice after a few days. Fancy/decorative exteriors (with things like dormers and staggered rooflines) should also be avoided because they really only provide more places for the roof to leak, more surface area for heat to escape, and a greater potential for severe storm damage to occur.

These types of common house structures could be made considerably more effective by first using the basement as an extremely large parking garage, thus saving land elsewhere. The rooftops of such facilities are also very large and thus could have many other potential applications if a flat roof was used instead. Such flat rooftops can have a tennis court (one of which uses as much land as five single-family homes), a landing area for flying cars, a massive greenhouse, a terrace/observatory, or a combination of all these things. Advocating as many extensive at-home businesses and fully featured recreational areas as I do, I obviously don't think it would be hard finding enough features to fill two or three extra floors. Martial arts schools, home schooling and research centers, libraries, offices, retail stores, and rooms to rent could all be added as well as enough bedrooms for residents that would make few other buildings in the community even necessary. Multistory buildings (4+) are absolutely essential for land conservation and look out of place only to those unconcerned with land conservation.

Common houses are essentially a botched concept!
Don't buy into them!

Appendix B:
Understanding Residential Parking Demands

Communal homes have substantially reduced parking areas. This takes into account the greater ability to work at home, the use of higher capacity vehicles, and the greater ability to carpool. With all the other necessities of the home competing for space on the ground floor, will the parking area that is provided be enough?

The concept of having our own household shuttle service, in which one resident runs errands, does the shopping, and drops people off at work, permits vehicle numbers to be cut down dramatically. On top of our work-at-home facilities, we are more self-sufficient and have many more fun things to do right at the home itself, which lowers the amount of travel required. These are all very important adaptations needed for communal living to work. However, residents have vacations, go away on day trips, they get called away for emergencies, and often go to a friend's house. Most of these activities do require individual transportation. But, how many parking spaces will be needed for a given number of people? Below are three categories that require us to offer individual transport. These calculations will be based on the theoretical transit needs of 100 working adults with 35 children.

Vacation Needs

The many advantages of communal living will hopefully lead to a situation where every working resident can enjoy five full weeks of vacation time each year, plus holidays. Not that bad, considering that we are also hoping for a shortened 32-hour workweek. All of this personal free time will place a high demand on the home's vehicles, so that residents can travel out to enjoy it all. We certainly all like to visit with friends and family as well as travel to various parks and tourist attractions. In a communal home, such get-away vacations will be much more possible, since other people are around to watch over things while you are away. Going away for vacation instead of staying home will also be essential to keep people living in such an intense environment from going a bit mad.

One hundred working adults would have 500 weeks of vacation time per year. Unless we were located in a very northerly climate, we should be able to spread most of these vacations out evenly over the year. With 52 weeks in a year, there would be an estimated 9.6 adults and 3.4 children away on vacation each week. Many of these 13 people will probably be traveling together as couples, friends, and as family units. Thus, out of 13 people, there would be about seven separate vacation parties to facilitate (two couples, two three-person groups, and three individuals). There may actually be less, as many people like to vacation together. Of these seven parties, it is my hope that at least three could use public transportation. Thus, we would ideally only need <u>four</u> cars and vans to facilitate travel—something that a single flying car may be able to do by itself one day. For every 100 people or so, there would also be a large RV for people to share, allowing everyone one full week of use a year. Because of possible overlaps (people going away for more than one week, and a heavier demand during the summer) we will assume the need for a total of five cars and vans, and one RV for every 100 working adults just for vacation.

Having a pool of five vacation cars and vans should cover all of our needs. Simply renting a car on an as-needed basis or making greater use of public transportation could handle any needs above and beyond this. It is also very important to note that most of these vacation-related vehicles will be out and away from the home at any given time. Cars returning from vacation on a Saturday evening would be right back out by Sunday morning. During this brief layover, when customer-parking demands are lower, these cars could temporarily park on the customer parking level (in some homes). Thus, to my surprise, the residential parking level hardly needs but a trace of parking space dedicated to this most demanding aspect of vacation travel.

Weekend Day and Overnight Trips

Before we begin this section, let's take some time to think about how often we ourselves go out on day and overnight trips. During the average year, I myself go to four or five two-day weekend workshops. Add in ten or so single-day workshops and basically I'm booked. The remaining 32 weekends of the year I basically do local activities for a few hours here and there and—like everyone else—take this time to get caught up on things and relax.

The point in reviewing our current weekend travels (for distances over, say, 20 miles) is that in a communal home, we can't all insist that we want to travel out each and every weekend, even though all the chores and shopping will be done ahead of time. This would break the bank, as it were. Instead, we should all expect to continue with our normal weekend routines and understand that the better we organize ourselves and the better the home designs become, the more we will gain over and above this norm.

In a home that has more activity areas than many small communities, where dozens of friends are right there to do things with, and (hopefully) where the local area has plenty of attractions nearby,[22] I really don't think this will be a problem. Such factors may even result in people staying home more often. We also have to remember that visiting friends and family is a two-way street: they come to us as much as we travel out to visit them. Thus, I'll assume that during an average summer, people might want to go out on a day-trip every other weekend and for two-day overnight trips, say, once a month. If the trip destination is within 20 miles, you could go out as much and for however long you wished by using the home's own shuttle system.

With 13 people away on vacation, there will be some 90 adults and 32 children at home during an average three-day weekend. This is a rather large number of people to facilitate weekend travel for. So, what we can do is organizing ourselves so that 65% of the home's residents work Monday to Thursday, while the other 35% (perhaps the non-customer-related craftspeople) work Friday to Monday. This would stagger demand. At this ratio, there would be a group of 59 adults and 21 children having their weekend between Friday and Sunday, and a second group of 31 adults and 11 children having their days off between Tuesday and Thursday.

---

[22] Hagerstown and Myerstown, Maryland are fairly ideal locations in the Tri-State area. They are located on the Appalachian foothills a mere ten minutes from the Appalachian Trail. There are seven State and National Forests within 20 miles, as well as the historic Antietam and Monocacy Civil War Battlefields to visit. Gettysburg, Washington DC, Baltimore, and the scenic Skyline Drive are one hour away! They are at an ideal road junction and well away from potential natural disasters. East Stroudsburg and Lebanon Pennsylvania are a couple other possible locations.

To arrange <u>distant</u> day and overnight travel for the larger Friday to Sunday group, we have to rely on the fact that people will go out on such trips only every other weekend. This allows us to divide the group into two. Counting five or so visitors that we invite along, that's <u>45</u> people each weekend to facilitate. This is still a lot of people. But here again, when we plan ahead and choose the right vehicles for the job, things become so much easier. For example, residents could consider investing in their own 50-passenger custom *charter coach!* Wow... wouldn't that be nice? Suddenly things seem so much clearer, right? Such a coach would actually cost less to purchase and operate than seven equivalent minivans. We would also want to have a smaller 20-passenger shuttle van for local commuting as well as weekend trips, too. Such shuttle vans and charter coaches could greatly augment weekend travel, to the point that few other vehicles may be needed. If the home were located in Hagerstown, Maryland, we'll say, a possible day and overnight trip schedule might look something like what is found on the next page.

Wow! As we can see from this extensive—yet hardly exhaustive—list, a shuttle van and a prearranged weekly schedule should more than facilitate even the most ambitious weekend travel plans. People wouldn't have to worry about driving, parking, or traffic and could enjoy the trip in the company of others. Such a coach could be customized with leather seating, tables, and a kitchenette. A home with 100 adults may even be able to own a six- to eight-passenger private plane.

In smaller multifamily homes, without such resources, it would take seven seven-passenger minivans in convoy to transport 45 people. This would take a lot more gas and seven times the number of drivers, but it would offer greater flexibility as the number of travelers fluctuates depending on the trip destination. It would also allow residents to hit up to seven separate destinations instead of just one.

If (as a study) we broke these 45 weekend travelers out into individual travel parties, we would find that there would normally be something on the order of 18 separate parties to facilitate. Such individualized travel needs could be handled by 13 Cars and 5 minivans overall. Taking public transportation or renting a car can handle circumstances beyond what is planned for. When including a shuttle van to transport 20 people to a specific preplanned destination, we could reduce the number of cars and vans needed from 18 to around ten. Basically, for every 100 people we would need one shuttle and 10 cars and minivans per weekend.

Long-Distance Commuting to an Outside Employer

The smaller the home, the greater this need will be. However, in larger facilities, few people would have to work at an outside job and fewer still will need to travel a great distance. Consider also that out of 100 working adults, 30% would work at home in support roles. Given such work facilities and an on-site support staff, it is hard to imagine the need for any more than, say, 20 needing to commute to work. Of these people, nearly all should be able to carpool or use our shuttle-taxi system. Thus, our overall commuting needs should only require about four or five cars and vans, and the use of the home's shuttle during the work week to drop people off. These vehicles would be away most of the time and actually could serve double duty as part of our fleet of weekend travel vehicles.

Sample Day and Overnight Shuttle Schedule (<u>two</u> trips per week):

01. Washington, DC attractions like the Smithsonian several times a year
02. The Catskill Mountains in New York
03. Pittsburgh attractions
04. One of many state and national parks such as the Allegheny National Forest
05. One of several zoos
06. Various sports events
07. Concerts
08. One of many regional lakes
09. Inner Harbor in Baltimore
10. The Marshal Space Flight Center, Maryland
11. War museums
12. The Reading Factory Outlets
13. The York Factory Outlets
14. Regional car, air, knife, and antique shows
15. Arts and crafts shows (where we may have a sales stand or two at ourselves)
16. Various fairs and festivals
17. A hunting/fishing excursion
18. Trips to ski resorts
19. The Appalachian Trail / Dehart Dam
20. A visit to other communal groups
21. Great Adventure Amusement Park – New Jersey
22. Gettysburg
23. A large wedding or social gathering
24. The Reading Rail Road Museum
25. The Altoona Living Colonial Settlers Museums
26. Philadelphia attractions
27. Hershey Amusement Park

There might be regular daily runs out to:
1. The library
2. The public pool
3. The shopping malls
4. Out for dinner to a local restaurant, with no parking worries
5. The movie theater
6. Historic and other downtown attractions
7. The ballpark or the athletic center

Sample Weekend (Two and Three-day) Shuttle/Charter Bus Schedule:
1. New York City attractions like the Museum of Natural History
2. Niagara Falls
3. The shore
4. The Great Lakes

Proportionately, if some of the home businesses fail, we could use what would have been the customer parking spaces for the additional cars we would then need to commute to outside jobs with. Ultimately, once our goal of having a paid-off home is realized, we would not have to work at any outside job that we did not want to.

In Summary – Vehicles Necessary Per 100 Working Adults:

Vacation Needs – One week or more:

Five cars and vans, and one RV would be needed. *Parking is needed only for two!*

Weekend Day and Overnight Trips:

One shuttle van and ten cars and minivans per weekend are needed. Vehicles would generally be available for daily commuting to work and for evening trips.

Long-Distance Commuting to an Outside Employer:

Three cars, two vans, and the use of the home's common shuttle van would be needed. Most of these cars can be used on weekends and all could be used for evening trips.

This totals: <u>nine</u> vans, <u>nine</u> cars, <u>one</u> shuttle van, and <u>one</u> RV (with optional charter coach) per 100 adults (three of these cars and vans are <u>always</u> out).[23] Another two cars and vans as well as the home's RV only stop at the home for about one day a week. Note: these parking bay figures do not include the parking needs of our business-related work trucks, which we also must provide room for.

---

[23] Note - These figures may change depending upon the home's location.

Appendix C:
Vehicle Bay and Driveway Features

The parking bay of large multifamily homes need to incorporate high-performance features and to remain free of clutter, so that this performance can be maintained. To help facilitate people moving in or out, for example, a variable-level truck dock can be added. Such an elevating dock can vary its height anywhere from the bay floor to a standard dock height (or even to the rafters) to aid in shipping and receiving activities. In the bay, there will be an overhead crane, sewer, power, water, and PC hookups for any electric cars or RVs parked in the garage. There will be in-wall outlets for air and power tools as well as lighting in the ceiling and walls. The bay will also be heated and over-pressurized to prevent outside contaminants from entering.

Garage Storage

Another prominent feature needed in the garage is storage areas for all the tools and equipment used to support work-related vehicles. There are many different types of service vehicles that home businesses can operate. Plumbers, electricians, construction workers, and repairpersons all require vehicles that are jam-packed with specialized equipment and tools that needs to be restocked and organized for proper operation. Storage areas would also be needed for things like child safety seats and seats removed from our minivans.

Removing all of the things that really don't belong in the garage is another way to consolidate its size. With so many residents, it is important to do this in order to keep things as organized and as smoothly flowing as possible. Mowers, yard tools, kids' bikes, and anything that you normally think to store in the garage, all have to be removed to prevent clutter from building up and slowing access in this high use area. In a specifically tailored multifamily home, a garage is also not the place for something like a small woodworking shop. Such shops must be given their own special area in the home and are, therefore, kept more orderly and functional. For those things that really are related to the garage, such as having a whole rack of brand new tires, I recommend either a garage closet or some form of indented storage area.

Garage closets can be great for those hard-to-place items that need a home somewhere. They can also be useful if the bay was not being used by vehicles. If the bay was converted into some sort of manufacturing facility, for example, such a closet could hold shop supplies and machinery. Closets can also serve as a conversion closet. Because these bays are so large and can be easily cleared out, they can potentially serve other functions. If you needed the bay as an emergency bed-down area for disaster victims, for example, the conversion closet would provide a place to store foldaway chairs, cots, and blankets until you needed them. When the time came, what was held neatly packed away in the closet could convert the entire garage into an unrecognizable shelter area.

Indents, which are the alternative to a garage closet, take the room out of the room and just provide raw floor-to-ceiling shelving space. The shelving units go back into the wall where they are tucked out of the way of where people are walking **(Figure 47 – Page 103).**

Exterior Closets

Consolidating what would have been many individual sets of lawn and garden tools into a single and more comprehensive set will be less expensive and gives residents the ability to more fully utilize a larger plot of land. With so many tools and various landscaping projects going on, it would have been hard to even think of using the back of the garage as a place to store such equipment. Not only would it be costly for someone carrying a shovel to accidentally put out a car window, but it would also bring a lot of dirt and still more people into the garage. Residents also need a place for a small agricultural tractor (one with mowing, tilling, hauling, and snow removal attachments), not just a riding mower. Such a tractor and equipment require a separate, more specialized place of their own.

Since none of these items ever get used in the garage or in the home for that matter, we need to use a method of storage that allows them to be accessed from the outside. Utility sheds usually serve this function, but they look shoddy, take up extra land, and are not very secure. By allocating a small portion of the home itself to serve as an exterior closet, we not only get something that looks better but something of much higher quality.

Exterior closets would have floor-to-ceiling storage racks ideal for lawn tools, bags of seed and fertilizer, as well as things like bicycles, driveway sealant, road salt, snow shovels and even bags of cement and bolt-on hurricane-proof window shields.

Driveway Options

As gridlock increases, our homes need to adjust their garage and driveway facilities from being geared for individual transportation to designs that match the specific needs of people who carpool and take mass transit to work. It is also crucial for communal homes to properly facilitate the arrival and departure of a greater number of residents and visitors.

Communal homes need to employ some kind of turning-circle or flow-through driveway that allow cars dropping people off to quickly turn around without having to back out onto a road. A motorized *lazy-susan rotating platform* (**Figure 29 – Page 85**) would essentially function the same way and would use less land.

Communal homes also need to employ a sheltered pick-up point and ground-level waiting rooms with bathrooms for customers and visitors. Due to the open communal nature of the home, this waiting area is also a necessary security precaution. Additional waiting areas are also needed for residents waiting for a ride who don't want to huddle under a small overhang or share an entrance that customers are using. When more people begin to carpool, such waiting areas will become essential.

Driveway Support

Driveways will have extensive features and shelving units to support driveway activities. There are power outlets and septic hookups for RVs. There is an outlet for air-operated tools and several power cord reels. There are hoses for general cleaning. There are vacuum hoses and tire inflation hoses that run from compressors and vacuums hidden in a supply room. There are fire extinguishers and medical kits. There are shelves for car care and maintenance items that also have to be prevented from cluttering up the garage. Over time, these conveniences really add up!

Appendix D:
Customer and Visitor Parking Needs

Home-based businesses are intended to generate income and help residents establish a level of self-sufficiency. Services like a small medical clinic or a hair salon would not be cost-effective, however, if they were just intended for residents. Even a great many residents, who would be potential clients and patients of such businesses, could not hope to fill the appointment books of such services to make them worthwhile. Attracting outside customers is vital to such homes!

To help draw in as many customers as we can, we must try to build in highly developed areas and locate ourselves near public transportation routs like a rail station and near the junction of intersecting bus routes. Locating near ideal road junctions that are by or between several cities is also important. Well over 100 such key locations exist nationwide. Building in such areas and spreading our facilities out across the entire country as much as possible will also help to get the word out about communal living.

The one problem with depending on outside customers, though, is that—in most cases—we need to provide them with a place to park. Providing them with a land-conscious parking garage apart from our own residential parking areas will be very expensive. Can such an added expense be lowered or avoided?

Is Having to Provide Customer Parking Avoidable?

Even if we could successfully draw in local clients by foot, I don't believe we would max out the potential of such businesses. We must remember that many private practices can remain open during evening hours; thus, doubling the number of patients and clients they could conceivably serve. Martial arts studios can themselves draw in large numbers of students at the same time. Thus, I don't believe it is possible to forgo customer parking.

If we lucked out and many of our neighbors did use our services, then such a parking garage could be used for other more important things like manufacturing or hydroponic food production. Thus, our investment in a customer-parking garage will never go to waste. The question then becomes how many parking spaces are needed?

How Many Customer Parking Spaces are Needed?

Some of the largest communal homes we've seen have so many services that it's as if they were the focal point of local businesses. The one nine-level design, for example, contains 16 offices for private practices, eight customer-related workrooms, four retail stores, a 20-person kung fu school, an 84-person convention center, an animal clinic, and even an automotive service center! Customers arriving for one of these many services would see—and likely use—many of the home's other services; thus, we are going to need a <u>lot</u> of customer parking spaces!

To estimate how many spaces are needed, we have to look at possible home businesses. Listed below are patient/client/student-oriented businesses. In parenthesis is the number of offices and the number of parking spaces they would likely require:

1. Attorney (3/.5)	**9.** Tailor (1/.5)	**17.** Beauty Salon (2/3)
2. Dental Practice (3/3)	**10.** Insurance Agent (1/.5)	**18.** Music Instruction (1/.5)
3. Optometrist (3/3)	**11.** Florist (1/.5)	**19.** Photo Studio (1/.5)
4. Acupuncture (3/3)	**12.** Dry Cleaning (1/.5)	**20.** Financial Services (1/.5)
5. Massage (2/3)	**13.** Architectural Firm (3/.5)	**21.** Auto Service Center (3/3)
6. Chiropractor (3/3)	**14.** Shoe Repair (1/.5)	**22.** Martial Arts School (3/20)
7. Veterinarian (3/3)	**15.** Tax Preparation (1/2)	**23.** Retail Store (1/3)
8. Goldsmith (2/.5)	**16.** Notary (1/.5)	**24.** Realtor (1/.5)

Although it is absolutely possible for the nine-level *Warhorse* design to offer **all** of these home businesses at the same time,[24] there is not enough parking available on the home's customer parking level (which only has 15 to 18 parking spaces) to support them. We would actually need <u>35</u> parking places for all of these services, and this still does not include our convention center's needs. Big drawing services such as the martial arts/yoga school are open largely after hours; thus, our nighttime parking requirements may be even worse than the day's. After-hours are also the best times for workshops and the home's retail stores. Our manufacturing businesses may also need to consider hiring outside employees to keep our businesses operating on a two- or three-shift rotation. Thus, we also have employee-parking demands to possibly consider.

It is important to note here that we may not be able to sustain so many businesses as we have listed here. Outside competition that is firmly established may be hard to compete with. Some of our businesses may only be seasonal and we may not have a complete set of residential skills needed to offer so many businesses.

Ways to Lower the Demand for Customer Parking

One of the best things we can do is organize days where a service would be strictly for the home's residents or neighbors to use, and to have different days for outside clients that travel in by car. In this way, we can cut parking demands by about 12 vehicles per day. Businesses may be asked to schedule light during a big conference. Large martial arts schools could put caps on the number of outside students (who require parking). And they may try to organize carpools or limit their classes to the weekends.

Visitor Parking Demands

In the smaller 42-bedroom home, where there were less extensive businesses, visitors are able to use the customer parking spaces after business hours. Such arrangements are not possible, though, in larger designs. Like customers, visitors may actually need their own parking level. To help lower visitor parking demands, visitors may be asked to come over mainly on the weekends and on holidays, when there aren't any customers and many residents are away on day trips. We may have two days a week set aside for visitors specifically, where we schedule customers lightly. With our shuttle service and our private plane perhaps, we may be able to give long-distance visitors a ride to and from our home.

---

[24] Such an extensive list doesn't include our work-vehicle-based businesses that the home could also have.

Appendix E:
The Engine Lab Shop Facility:

The process of dismantling a contemporary engine and rebuilding or overhauling it is obviously an involved process. Mechanics must utilize a host of tools and parts, which—after a short time—begin to clutter up their work area. Although the mechanic working on the project may not feel they are disorganized, the shop is essentially frozen until the completion of the project. Anyone else wishing to use the workbench is likely to misplace or scatter the parts and tools the other is working with.

A basic shop's rectangular layout usually results from having to adapt an existing room, such as part of a basement or garage, to serve as a shop. Such general all-purpose layouts are inadequate for the involved and more specialized work we hope to perform in the sub-industrial-scale shops of a true multifamily home. If we wish to work at home and utilize its potential to replace most forms of business that society depends on (and travels to), we'll need more than just a corner of a basement to perform our tasks in.

Shop Function and Layout

Shops are much more dynamic than people realize, and for them to function as anything much more than just a basic assembly area or crafts shop requires adding definition (specialization). Shops are dynamic for a number of reasons. They are made up of: **(1)** A shelving area. **(2)** A workbench area with drawers, fire suppression, scanning devices and a computer workstation that enables mechanics to review schematics and interface with the home's central computer. A camera could also record the work being done for training purposes. **(3)** Ample wall space for different types of equipment such as a miter or radial saws to be placed against. **(4)** Open floor space for other equipment. **(5)** Open floor space is needed to assemble/dismantle, clean, and to finish (paint or stain) a project. **(6)** Storage for project materials and parts. **(7)** Trash for scraps and fluids. **(8)** Proper lighting and heavy duty power outlets. **(9)** Good ventilation. **(10)** Safety features such as a medical kit and an eye rinse sink. Shops are also a place that can get pretty dusty and smelly, and can even be somewhat dangerous. Not only is there an excess of power tools, but you often have sparks and pieces of wood and metal flying around.

From the above list, we can see several things that do not belong together. Number 5 (where things get painted and cleaned with strong paints and solvents, and where a dismantled motor could be laying around for weeks) seems to be something that needs to be isolated. If you were making a canoe, for example, you would need a place for a partially constructed canoe and a place to manufacture individual components. Separating the component shop from a smaller assembly area would allow us to divide the shop into several more specialized rooms, and also adds more wall space. The workbench area (where the most intricate and detailed work is preformed) also needs to be separated to keep technicians and electronics safely away from the main work area, (the center of **Figure 23 on page 56** is an ideal example).

This approach to shop design has several advantages. It keeps the work area neater. It enables someone looking for a specific tool to go to the workbench area instead of having to hunt through a project area, where they may kick a part or bump into someone busy with delicate or even dangerous work. Any sparks, dust, fumes, or bright light (welding) coming from the work area are also prevented from flowing into the workbench and shelving areas, where things could catch fire.

Removable shelving trays (much as you find pre-made pizza sitting on in a pizza parlor) can allow mechanics to pull parts off in the order that they need to be put back on and then, once the tray is full, place it into a tall multi-tray rack for safe keeping. Thus, the shop can remain useful for other projects. The 90 cm deep built-in floor-to-ceiling shelving units in the shop should be watertight, enabling the whole area to be hosed out. These shelving units provide storage for paper towels, forms, tags, cleaning solvents, part bins (overstocked and color-coordinated), and other equipment. Indents between the shelves and benches can be made large enough for rollaway tool cabinets/bins (which can be pulled out and transported), compressor bins, shop vacuums, and welding canisters/bins. A small coat closet is also needed for visiting mechanics to place their coats and toolboxes. When called upon, a mechanic can just grab their toolbox and coat and be on the move.

There may be indents provided to keep carts, dollies, and hand trucks out of the way along the hallways. Any 90-degree hallway junction could be rounded off so that it is easier to move carts down them. There may be a closet for heavy-duty dumpsters, too. Dumpsters form an integral part of the work area and our policy to scavenge for anything (any circuit and bolt) that is still useful. They help keep the work area clean of the boxes, crates, Styrofoam, and plastic packaging that new components come in.

Manufacturing Complex Components

"Casting quality metal and rubber parts that cannot be found for an old car or that are missing from an antique ourselves, may be the only way to restore the functionality and the value to an item that maybe worthless otherwise."[25] Casting and tooling a new part or components is difficult, but there is a growing potential to do this effectively from even a small shop. This potential largely comes from the use of computer software such as AutoCAD, which enables a person to download a part's schematics from the Internet, design a part themselves, or use laser radar to accurately scan an old part right into the computer. Once there, a product called SmartStart can take this AutoCAD file and render a detailed three-dimensional plastic part (in a microwave-like device) that is then used to make a mold.[26] The furnaces needed to produce molten metal for such a mold are not much bigger than a refrigerator, which is easy to find a place for. Many other industrial tooling machines are also small enough to fit into these sub-industrial-scale shops without modification. The process used for the fabrication of composites can also allow our shops to build things like custom-made mountain bikes and canoes, too.

---

[25] How to Cast Small Metal and Rubber Parts
[26] Popular Mechanics – August 1997

Appendix F:
Costs Saved by Working at Home

Below is a series of five categories that must be considered as part of the overall cost involved in traveling to work: expenses that we don't really think about but that add up over time. In these calculations, we consider the cost saved by eight residents working from home. The calculations are based on an average one-way travel time of 25 minutes (just below my office's average of 29 minutes each way).

Instead of spending time on the road traveling to work, these eight residents could be earning an income of about $12 an hour:

Time Saved:	Dollar Value:
33.3 hours per week	400 dollars
1632 hours per year (68 days)	19,584 dollars
2,040 days per 30 years	***588,000 dollars***

Adding to this is the cost of owning a vehicle. Figuring that two of the eight residents would probably be able to carpool, we calculate what it costs for the six remaining residents to drive to work in terms of the actual vehicle costs. Based on an average commuting distance of 20 miles one-way and a total cost of a vehicle (after interest) of $20,000, each of the six residents who drove to work could be expected to go through a new car every 14 years if the car was used just for work:

In Cars:	In Dollars:
6 cars in 14 years	120,000 dollars
12.9 cars in 30 years	***258,000 dollars***

Estimated savings in gas would be $22,680 per decade and ***$68,040*** per 30-year period: if each car got 35 mpg and the cost for a gallon of gas was $1.35.

If each car went through three sets of tires costing $200 per set, averaged $1,200 in repairs, and used $260 worth of oil, filters, plugs, and wiper blades, the estimated savings would be $12,360 over a 14-year period and ***$26,574*** over a 30-year period.

Lastly, if each driver paid an average of $150 less in insurance premiums each year (because they traveled less), the savings would be ***$27,000*** per 30-year period.

In total, over a typical 30-year mortgage period, the savings included in these categories would add up to ***$967,614.00!*** This is $32,253 in savings each year! This level of savings certainly justifies the purchase of a fully featured communal home that has the shop, project, and office facilities necessary to make our extensive home-based businesses work. It also prevents the pollutants of some 50,000 gallons of gas from being expelled into the environment, not to mention all of the tires, parts, and ultimately dozens of rundown vehicles! Additionally, you wouldn't have to put up with the hassle of commuting, or all the dangers involved in traveling to work, especially when there's poor weather.

Appendices G: Space Utilization in Top Four Designs

	4-Bedroom Home	7-Bedroom Home	+%	11-Bedroom Home	+%	23-Bedroom Home	+%
Number of Bedrooms	4	7	**75%**	11	**57%**	23	**109%**
Land Used	146.8m²	203.7m²	38.8%	317.6m²	55.9%	489.6m²	54%
Land Use Per Bedroom	36.7m²	29.1m²	-21%	28.9m²	-.7%	21.3m²	-26%
Work Related:							
Shop Space	16.3m²	31.9m²	96%	47.9m²	50.2%	186m²	288%
Office Space	16.3m²	25.3m²	55.2%	46m²	81%	105m²	123%
Waiting Room Capacity	-NA-	-NA-	-0-	3	100%	8	166%
Reception Desk Area	-NA-	-NA-	-0-	4.2m²	100%	5.0m²	20%
Craft and Project Area	16.3m²	24.7m²	51.5%	24.4m²	-1.3%	73m²	199%
No. of Work Vehicles	1	2	100%	2	-0-	3	50%
Recreational Related:							
Living Room Area	16.3m²	35.4m²	117%	52.8m²	49.2%	93.5m²	77%
Game Room Space	22.0m²	28.4m²	29%	23.9m²	-16%	80m²	235%
Exercise/Weight Space	9.8m²	13.0m²	32.6%	12.9m²	-.7%	23.5m²	82%
Open Martial Arts Space	-NA-	-NA-	-0-	28.8m²	100%	51.8m²	80%
Music Room Space	-NA-	-NA-	-0-	-NA-	-0-	27.5m²	100%
Rooftop Patio/Landing	20m²	63.0m²	315%	68.4m²	8.6%	96m²	40%
Terrace Area	-NA-	16.7m²	100%	24.8m²	48.5%	24.2m²	-2.5%
Library Shelf Capacity	956 Books	1,630 Books	70.5%	6,626 Books	400%	3,968 Books	-40%
Dirt Bike/Snow Mobile	2	2	-0-	2	-0-	6	200%
Support Related:							
Garage Footprint	55.0m²	90.1m²	63.8%	120.4m²	33.6%	212.6m²	76.5%
Vehicle Seating Capacity	7	15	114%	26	73.3%	42	61.5%
Visitor Capacity	8	12	50%	16	33.3%	32	100%
Visitor Office Capacity	-NA-	2	100%	-NA-	-100%	5	100%
Kitchen Area	8.5m²	13.0m²	52.9%	18.5m²	42.3%	40.0m²	116%
Dining Room Capacity	6	8	33.3%	12	50%	12	-0-
Home Office Area	-NA-	7.9m²	100%	8.5m²	8.1%	5.28m²	-38%
Bulk Storage Space PB	5.6m² (Attic)	5.7m²	1.8%	4.9m²	-14%	6.0m²	22.4%
Conversion Closet Area	-NA-	-NA-	-0-	-NA-	-0-	57.5m²	100%
Greenhouse Area PB	9.4m² (Attic)	7.1m²	-25%	9.7m²	36.6%	14.1m²	46%
Toilets/Showers PB	.75/.5	1.0/.43	—	.91/.45	—	.96/.52	—
Ave. Dist. Bed to Bath	2.3m	3.6m	—	3.2m	—	5.4m	—
Hall and Stairwell Width	1.05m	1.05m	—	1.5m	—	1.4m	—
Ave Dist Bed to Steps	4.8m	4.2m	—	5.4m	—	8.4m	—
Elevator Capacity	1	1	-0-	4	300%	12	200%
Phone Booths	0	1	100%	0	-100%	5	100%
Average Increase			57.7%		48.6%		92.7%

PB = Per Bedroom, +% (gray columns) = Percent increase over previous design
Metric Conversion: meters square X 10.76 = square feet, meters X 3.28 = feet

Analysis: This is a general comparison of the number and size of various work, recreation, and support areas within each home. The number and size of such areas should generally keep pace with the increase in the number of bedrooms each successive home has. The table does not address all facets of a design. Smaller homes that don't have a music room or an open martial arts training area, per say, should be able to use other areas for these purposes. There may be offsetting features or other organizational workarounds to compensate for certain shortages and—because of the aspect of economy of scale—some areas don't need to be proportional in size to the number of residents. Each design will have it's own strengths and weaknesses. The last 23-bedroom *Concurrence* home design is my most recommended facility given society's current eco/economic situation.

Appendix H: Emergency-Enhanced Features

Modern society has certainly embraced all of the modern conveniences that the last century had to offer. Everything from home computers and televisions to refrigerators and indoor toilets have all become standard household amenities. However, as our homes have increased in their value, little has changed about their *inability* to cope with a disaster. Unfortunately, disasters never go away and the ever-increasing size of our communities only makes their affects that much worse. As the climate gradually becomes warmer, one can best bet on even more seasons of severe weather.

Apart from doing our best to avoid untenable locations **(Figure 51)** that are constantly under threat of disasters or other potential problems, we must consider building our homes doubly beyond the local codes (which officials are pressured to keep to a minimum) to better cope with such events. Homes—wherever they are located—last far too long to simply hope that things will be okay forever.

Homes can be improved in very practical and functional ways. The following is a list of basic enhancements that almost anyone can incorporate into a new home:

- Homes need a more basic square or octagonal shape (which have greater internal volume for a given amount of exterior wall length) to lower the amount of surface area exposed to the heat of summer and the cold of winter. These shapes also lower a home's wind resistance.

- Open living areas (like the undivided kitchen, dining, and living room section of a home) need to be walled off into individual rooms. Not only does this add more wall length for the placement of furniture and lower noise levels throughout the home, it's structurally more stable and prevents a damaged outer wall or broken window from adversely affecting the entire home. It prevents the rapid spread of fire and smoke and allows unused rooms to be closed off to conserve the heat and air-conditioning.

- A double-door, mudroom-type breezeway entrance helps conserve heat, adds security and flexibility, and prevents pets from inadvertently getting out. Having a bathroom by this entrance would also prevent people who may have been working in muddy or contaminated conditions from having to track through the home just to use the bathroom.

- Instead of extravagant formal living areas and an overly large master bedroom, all bedrooms in the home should be more equal in size, have more acceptable amounts of closet space, and be as widely separated as possible. Thus, if your children or displaced family members are forced to move in with you after a disaster, it won't be such an inconvenience. Slightly smaller master bedrooms are also easier to heat.

- A 10 x 17 spare bedroom can be specifically designed to have up to four bunk beds placed in each corner of the room. Such a high-capacity eight-person bedroom would be a great help to family and friends during mass evacuations. Such rooms keep sleeping guests quietly out of the way so that home operations can continue as normal without interruption.

- Bathrooms should be handicap-accessible and segmented into separate shower rooms and half baths as much as possible. This allows all the functions of a bathroom to be used simultaneously—without any loss of privacy—if there's an overflow of people in the home.

- Apart from stairs, a multi-level home can have actual fire pole or ladder shafts to escape from a fire or to get to lower floors in the home on a daily basis much more quickly.

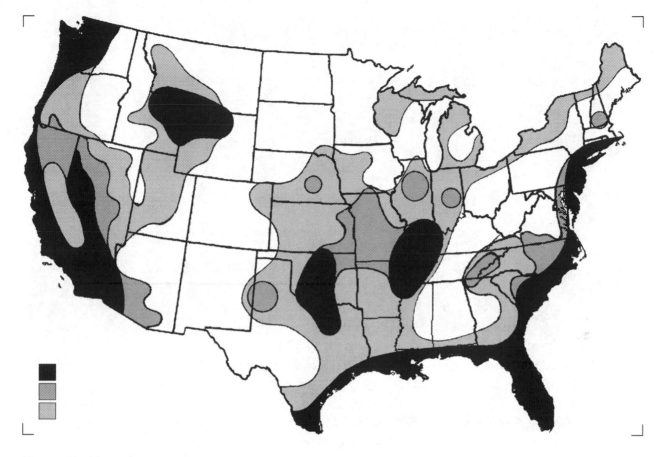

Figure 51: Too often, people make the assumption that it's OK to live in a dangerous area because *all* areas have risks. Although this is true in a limited sense, some areas are far more dangerous than others. In this map, I've estimated the degree of danger to residents from 20 problems and potential disasters:

Hurricanes	Sea-level rise	Acute hail and rain	Poor air quality
Flood-prone areas	Tsunami potential	Acute snowfall	Toxic pollution
Earthquakes	Volcanic activity	Excessive cold	Excessive nuclear power
Tornados	Derecho thunderstorms	Drought conditions	Mining related problems
High heat and humidity	Acute lightning	Acute insect problems	Strategic annihilation

Areas shown in black are the most hazardous, while areas in white are relatively trouble free. Overall, the potential problems facing the eastern and gulf seaboards seem to be the most numerous. In the 100 years or so between major CA earthquakes, there could be over 700 Atlantic hurricanes. Hurricanes are exceptionally dangerous in hot and humid areas that are overly dependent on power lines to provide AC. Sections of this region suffer from earthquakes, tornados, flooding, excessive termites and ticks, acute lightning, a heavy concentration of nuclear power plants, numerous Superfund sites, and poor air quality. There is also the danger of rising sea levels and a potential Canary Island-generated tsunami in this area!

Although relatively unknown, the SE Missouri area is not only extremely flood-prone with the ever-present danger of tornados it's also a region susceptible to extreme earthquakes. The NW Wyoming region is not only very cold and exceptionally earthquake-prone it's also the home of the Yellowstone super volcano, which is geologically overdue for an eruption sometime in the next few thousand years. The West Coast has well-known earthquake and volcanic problems, as well as being prone to flooding, mudslides, wildfires, poor air quality, and extreme heat and droughts in certain areas. The other shaded areas have similar, though less sever, problems. In the end, we must remember that although we have the engineering know-how to build almost anywhere, few communities build to such standards and no one wants to live in a disaster zone. Be smart, live safe, and look for areas with the potential for solar and wind power generation!

- Year-round rooftop greenhouses can produce ten times more vegetables than a garden of equal area. They need less water, get more sunlight, eliminate soil erosion, need fewer—if any—pesticides, and help us to avoid widespread food contamination.

- Homes need to have rainwater-holding cisterns located around the home or out under the driveway. Such cisterns, which can be as simple as a barrel or as large as your living room, can capture hundreds of gallons of Giardia-free drinking water every time it rains.

- Avoid central-air and heating units that require extensive ventilation ductwork. Heat can be better controlled with small and efficient tabletop ceramic heaters that are much easier to replace than structurally damaged ductwork or a large central unit.

- Emphasis should be placed on lowering the amount of plumbing in the home so that it's easier to maintain, less likely to freeze without heat, and so that the hot water does not have to run so long before it gets warm. More access panels are required to service the plumbing and electrical systems throughout the home.

- Large bay windows should be avoided in favor of smaller windows that are more standard in size (for easy replacement) and protected with screens (which need to be interwoven with heavier gauge wire). Windows should be sold with their own bolt on, custom-fitting window shields to protect them like shutters used to before they just became ornaments.

- Heavier garage doors that swing open are needed.

- There is a definite need for garage closets to eliminate clutter. This way if the garage door is blown out, residents won't have all their things exposed to the elements.

- Garages should be large enough to protect vehicles as wide as an ambulance or as long as an extended-cab pickup truck. Such vehicles form the basis of many service-oriented plumbing and electrical businesses that are needed in times of recovery.

- For long-term durability, use concrete-filled structural support walls in the basement (instead of just support beams), steel floor joists that don't rot or mildew, and use only the highest strength concrete in the home's foundation and basement walls! Octagonal-shaped walls are also stronger when coping with ground pressure or the shockwave of an earthquake.

- For energy efficiency, sound insulation, and added security, you can use heavier exterior-type doors within the home and fill interior walls with insulation. Such added insulation could allow smaller rooms to be heated with nothing more than a light bulb.

- Homes should have extensive storage space worked into every nook-and-cranny: in the staircase, in the floor between floor joists, in overhead compartments running throughout the home and hallways, and on massive shelving units built over the bed. Built-in, wall-to-wall and floor-to-ceiling furnishings offer four to ten times more storage capacity than decorative end tables and nightstands. The attic should be finished off for storage and the basement ceiling should be a standard height for full, semi-protected usage.

- In order to save water during droughts, a home can have water-free urinals and a gray water recycling system that uses the shower and sink water to flush the toilets. Consider also having a composting toilet in the home even if it's just for emergency use.

- To save energy on heating and cooling and to make more room available for more critical features, the dining room could be reduced in size to be nothing more than a six- to eight-seat restaurant-like dining booth or dining bar by the kitchen.

- All homes should have a small wheelchair elevator for the elderly and for those recovering from an injury. You may also want to consider placing a 220-volt outlet in a bedroom in order to potentially support medical devices.

- The home's rain gutters can be greatly enhanced to serve like a protective steel frame around the home. Like roll bars on a car, they can help protect the home from falling tree limbs!

- Small home offices, with powerful home computers and equipment, should be securely housed in rooms with heavier internal walls that are wrapped in a protective waterproof membrane in case of roof damage. Windows should generally be avoided in such rooms.

- We should avoid having ill-protected outdoor lawn sheds. By incorporating an <u>exterior</u> closet into the lines of the home itself, we can have a much more secure structure (as strong as the home itself) to prevent unnecessary damage to valuable equipment.

- Basements should avoid using insecure and inefficient window wells.

- Space for an extra freezer unit is potentially helpful.

- Home sprinkler systems are needed and everyone should own a fire extinguisher and a large end table-size fireproof safe to secure money and documents during a crisis.

- To support extensive hiking, mountain biking, camping, and hunting activities, the home could use a dedicated camping support room with gear racks, a bike maintenance shop, and an internal ready-up area.

- Because trash may go uncollected for weeks, we need a separate garage closet for twice as many garbage cans as we normally need.

- A two-line phone system can give families an edge in reacting to breaking events.

- The shrubs and trees around our homes should have an edible or medicinal quality (such as maple and oak trees). Maple leaves and acorns are edible, the sap of a maple tree is a well-known emergency water source, and boiled oak leaves release tannic acid, a strong backwoods antiseptic. Having a compost bin helps to regenerate outdoor gardens, too.

- Unless you live in Tornado Alley, things like a survival bunker or fallout shelters are hardly necessary or even all that desirable. Such "emblems of fear" and misunderstanding have been rightfully avoided by mainstream Americans.

The 1999 Hurricane Season: A premonition of what was to come

Although hit four times in 2004, Florida wasn't the only place to be repeatedly hit by back-to-back hurricanes. During a seven-week period in 1999, North Carolina was itself hit by Hurricanes Dennis, Floyd, and Irene as well as Tropical Storm Harvey. Accumulated rainfall topped **four** feet in places! Although Dennis actually backtracked to hit NC twice, Floyd caused the most damage. Its unpredictable path and early **Category 5** wind speeds (which "skinned trees like bananas" in the Bahamas)[27] forced the evacuation of 2.6 million residents from as far south as Florida. 30,000 homes were flooded and millions lost power. Floodwaters—reaching 20 to 31 feet beyond flood stage—also inundated **209** waste treatment plants, 22 water treatment plants, and closed **300** roads. Fouled by more than 100,000 rotting livestock carcasses, floating sewage, industrial chemicals and pesticides, and leaking petroleum, such floodwaters quickly became a major health risk. Weeks of runoff eventually created a 350-square-mile dead zone in Palmico Sound, the nation's second largest coastal estuary. By the time Irene hit in October, resident Leroy Johnson noted, "People had nothing left to lose!" In all, there was a record breaking five Category 4 hurricanes in 1999!

---

[27] Michelle Rolle, a resident of Abaco, NC as reported on MSNBC.com – September 17th, 1999.

Appendix I:
Ten Ways to Save the Environment: <u>Now</u>

All of the normal efforts of recycling, carpooling, and land conservation can only go so far. There is a lot more we can do, but this does not mean that we have to do without. If we all make a concerted and deliberate effort to do things right, we can easily achieve both an increase in our quality of living as well as a greatly lessened impact on the land. Apart from communal living, the following is a list of ten additional items that would greatly benefit the environment and our own lives in the process:

1. Functionality

Functionality is the gemstone of society's know-how! To me, this aspect is even a more important concept to convey than things like communal living, because communal living is a byproduct of designing something (a home) more functionally. Overall wastefulness is avoided when we achieve functionality because designs are more effectively put to use to perform a more defined task. This is the definition of efficiency. Our society certainly has the know-how to design a product with an uncanny ability to perfectly suit our needs if we want it to. If we choose to forgo functional designs because we aren't willing to foot the bill or want something that looks fancy, we only end up hurting ourselves and our environment in the process.

To me, functionality has an inherent beauty **(Figure 52).** For example, the reasons I think so many of us love (and study about) modern and historic military weapons is not because we are all killers in want of destruction. It's because such weapons (as well as more benign things like race cars) are designs that are ***purpose-built***—dedicated machines that truly excel at what they were meant to do! The fact that they're for war isn't what attracts us. It is their embodiment of serious thought and functionality that is so enticing, but which is so lacking in other parts of our everyday, humdrum society. Would a tank sport frillies and other wasteful, non-critical aesthetics like a false hood-scoop or spoilers? No, of course not. Our clamor for aesthetics is the opposite: a false desire geared more for displaying wealth in a class system than it is a true call for the effective application of design.

A home is not the place to be trying to make some sort of social statement. Homes are, plain and simply, our only hope to guarantee private, productive, and serviceable living conditions. If you don't happen to like a functional home's natural appearance, then don't cut down so many of the trees around it!

2. Product Standardization

One of the most immediate solutions available to us to reduce waste is that of product standardization: a policy of limiting the sheer number of competing products in the same category to the most ideal ones. Such a policy can be applied to any product we use in our daily lives. We could standardize the air filters, sparkplugs, and even the engines that our subcompact cars use, which would increase the availability of parts and speed repairs. We could even choose to employ a better engine overall because the sheer numbers of them

The Analytical Design Process

In general, it's not hard to design something. All designs have their supporting reasons for why they are the way they are. But this leaves us to ask what makes any one design better than any other. Why is it, for example, that small countries like Sweden have a better jet fighter (the JAS 39) than larger countries like America, who have far more money to spend? Why are Soviet or Israeli tanks so different from American tanks even though both countries could have made an M-1 copy if they wanted to? It's important to understand what makes a good design good if we are to adapt quickly and efficiently.

Ultimately, all designs involve give-and-take: a balancing act that trades one virtue for another. Heavy armor (to continue the military analogy) trades mobility for survivability, while light armor trades survivability to gain mobility and exploit enemy weaknesses. Ultimately (by definition), the best designs are those that are the most suitable for their expected operating conditions, the most appropriate for their intended purpose, and those that are both effective and efficient at what they do.

The analytical design process helps to identify the best possible design solutions for a given problem by looking at every possible consideration. There is: **(A)** a thorough analysis of the overall problems being experienced. **(B)** An understanding of history, available technology, and any constraints that limit what overall solutions can be employed. **(C)** A <u>concise</u> and realistic understanding of the operating conditions to be expected. **(D)** The creation of an overall strategy or policy (covering all aspects of a particular problem, not just bits and pieces of it) to help govern all the individual solutions being planned. **(E)** An understanding of all available options, including what the ideal solution would be regardless of cost. **(F)** The establishment and careful balancing of set requirements where everything is considered a factor to be weighed accordingly. **(G)** Then, there is the laborious and very deliberate structuring of resources into individual designs whose individual attributes are proportional to one another and that do not overlap the qualities present in other designs. **(H)** Together, these individual solutions form a streamlined system without the wasteful duplication of effort. This type of structuring is typical of a military doctrine which tailors one weapon to perform a specific function in an overall strategy, while relying on other weapons to perform their given tasks. Overall, the goal is to explicitly pinpoint a specific niche or role for a design to fulfill based on what it is trying to accomplish. Invariably, it usually takes more than one design to solve a problem. This is because using several designs to perform specific functions, rather than trying to devise one design that attempts to do everything itself, generally leads to efficiency and more robust performance.

Simply put, by understanding how the process of analytical design is supposed to work by seeing how it is used in other areas (like the military, mountaineering or in racing) where so much performance is demanded, we can apply these very same principals to better design the everyday things we use in the rest of our humdrum society. If we can design our homes, cars, clothing, and all of our belongings to perfectly suit our needs, there will be nothing we cannot do and nothing that could ever stop us!

Thinking About How We Think

The ancient Chinese actually had a way to instill further creativity into those who think they had already achieved some ultimate solution. They said that whenever you create something, ask yourself three additional questions: **1.** Why does it work? **2.** How does your answer speculate (in very specific ways within the given design)? **3.** What are its limits (on a very broad perspective regarding what can ultimately be achieved)? Thus, one could argue that if the Wright Brothers had asked themselves these three questions, they should have at least been able to speculate about the possibility of something like an Airbus A380.

Interestingly, the Chinese also had a way to tell if you had a good idea or not. They said, the more that what you say makes others angry, the more you know you're right! This hints at how societies invariably become **complacent** over time and, therefore, agitated when confronted with change. Einstein himself echoed this very same sentiment when he said, *"If at first an idea is not considered absurd, it has no chance of succeeding,"* which again shows how a complacent society often reacts to change. In stark contrast, 17th-century Holland (a small country forced to live by its wits) was a perfect example of how an open society (which not only allowed free inquiry, but fully promoted it) can flourish into an economic powerhouse!

Figure 52 (Courtesy Daimler Benz): Functionally speaking, the Mercedes A-Class micro car has most cars beaten! Despite its diminutive size (only 11.8 feet in length), the A-Class offers a five-passenger seating capacity and it has an extraordinary cargo carrying ability. All four of its passenger seats can either be folded down or <u>completely</u> removed. As seen at bottom, when all of the seats are removed, it leaves a completely open and <u>flat</u> cargo floor available—running front to back. This allows items ranging from surfboards to mountain bikes to be easily carried within! The A-Class is sized more closely to the needs of an individual commuter with a long drive ahead of them. It's easy to park and maneuver, gets incredible mileage **(52 mpg),** and has the quality and safety of a Mercedes Benz! Mercedes is also now testing a purely hydrogen-powered version.

being produced would reduce the engine's cost. Using the best available consumer information, we should ultimately try to limit the ridiculous number of cars competing for the same market niche by focusing our spending dollars on just two or three particular models that are rated the best overall in each class.

Due to their sheer numbers, homes can also multiply even minor improvements into tremendous savings. Just standardizing the type of light bulbs we use can have far reaching advantages. E-Lamps, OLEDs, or advanced fluorescent bulbs use about one-third the amount of power as conventional fixtures and last ten to 25 times longer. Multiply these savings by the estimated 1.5 billion light sockets across the U.S. and you could reduce overall air pollution dramatically.[28] Thus, instead of allowing the cheapest products to be sold to those unwilling to spend the extra buck for something more efficient, we could use the sheer numbers of these higher quality items to greatly curb our overall wastefulness. I also don't believe that this would stagnate innovation because the scientists and specialists in these research departments and laboratories are all pretty much paid the same amount, regardless. It may even speed innovation as key products are refined and tested more often.

3. Multilevel Buildings and Roadways

In many ways, we already have the answer to our environmental problems: buildings. Taller buildings not only conserve land, they serve to condense things. Part of the reason we have so many roads and why it takes so long to get places is that things are so spread out. Sprawling, one-level shopping centers and schools should at least be built over a commercial parking garage. Much as in Europe, small communities could even share a central multilevel parking garage that eliminates the need for streets, driveways, and garages to be built within the community for every home. Automated parking garages, which use elevators to stack cars in a silo 15 to 20 high, need very little land. Over 100 cars can be parked in the area of a traditional 10-car parking lot (example: www.spacesaverparking.com).

Roads use more land than our homes and shopping malls do and we need to make more use of this land as well. Below an ordinary roadway's surface, we could have an accessible tunnel for sewer, power, phone, and waterlines. Most such utilities are already under roadways, but not within any sort of tunnel-like structure where they can be maintained or upgraded without excavation. Having more condensed and self-contained communities would also lower the vastness of these networks.

Building large platforms over a roadway (perhaps with our sewer, water, and power system suspended underneath) is another possibility. Such platforms can support a monorail system (for passengers, freight, and trash), recreational areas like basketball courts, and extensive greenhouse facilities. Platforms can also be used over individual driveways with gardens and shrubs planted on top.

4. Vigorously Fighting Forest Fires and Illegal Poaching

Taking active measures to protect our planet's ecology and the delicate cyclic balances within it can include the direct protection of our forests and wildlife by vigorously confronting forest fires and illegal poaching. If our planet is warming and droughts begin

---

[28] Popular Mechanics – September 1992

hitting places (such as rainforests) harder and harder, we will need to develop a large and highly specialized international fire fighting force. By funding and equipping forestry fire fighters as well as we do an army air-born division, we can battle blazes anywhere in the world at the drop of a hat. To this end, we need far better fire bombing aircraft than those in use today and perhaps even heavy-lift VTOL aircraft able to support operations in the most remote and hard to reach wildernesses.

To help support the operations of these regionally shifting units, large national parks can build relatively unseen support facilities right into their park's visitor center: areas that remain closed off until they are needed. Remote ranger stations could also be designed to support operations to stop illegal poaching. Using unmanned aerial reconnaissance drones that takeoff and land vertically, rangers can quickly scan mountainous and wooded areas by air for the infrared body heat of poachers or a lost party.

5. Computerized Traffic-Control Networks

With so many vehicles, we almost have to work within this existing framework to improve things in the near term. One of the best ways to do this is to improve our traffic control systems like Atlanta did when it was preparing for the Olympic games. They decided that they would need a network (complete with cameras at key intersections) able to control all the traffic lights from a central headquarters. Controlling traffic like this is absolutely critical! Mistimed traffic lights can be totally backwards to the actual flow of traffic, wasting thousands of man-hours and gallons of fuel a day. We can all do what we can to help speed things up at lights by not leaving so much space between cars as we pull out and perhaps even by simply going though a light (after we've stopped, of course) when no one else is coming. Nationwide, I also believe we could eliminate 400,000 unnecessary stop signs and I would definitely consider the elimination of **all** highway billboard signs.

6. Fewer Restaurants and Gas Stations

Part of our environmental problem stems from the capitalistic ideals that find three competing gas stations sitting on three of the four corners of an intersection. What's wrong with this picture? Restaurants are also very wasteful to land! They are all one-level buildings with equally wasteful one-level parking lots. We must realize that we don't actually need different restaurants to get a wider selection of food. Any seafood place can cook a burger and fries! Any burger place can make a roast beef sandwich! Apart for about five hours a day, restaurants are practically empty 75% of the time. If you wouldn't want to work in one of these places, then don't go to them and expect others to either!

7. Making Products and Consumables at Home

Has anyone stopped to ask why we have so many damn clothing stores? Seventy-five percent of the area used at our shopping malls is basically just for clothing. You could easily make a good pair of pants or a jacket in about 12 to 25 hours. Making our own clothes on a community-wide scale can eliminate the need for so many department stores that hinge on the fact that you are too busy working for someone else to provide for your own needs. Underpaid and mistreated employees very often manufacture store-bought clothing items. It may be cheaper to simply buy something at a store, but doing so literally supports a brutal—often illegal—industry.

8. Delivering Groceries

In the case of supermarkets, it would be far better (if the quality of service and produce could be ensured) to have our groceries delivered to our homes. Everyone generally hates to shop anyway, so instead of having to travel to the store (which then needs to provide large customer parking areas and shopping aisles that are broad enough for shoppers) we should home deliver orders. Alternately, we could have a drive-up pickup dock where people could be underway in less than a few minutes. To facilitate this service, canned goods and groceries of all kinds would need to be indexed and packaged for automated storage and retrieval. Durable and reusable plastic shipping containers (bins) would replace disposable grocery bags.

9. Living More Simply

The following is a summary checklist of over 160 conservation tips that can dramatically help us to improve the environment on an individual level:

Water Conservation
* Take navy showers, turning the water off as you lather up
* Shower less often. Every second or third day is just fine
* Take sponge baths whenever possible
* Catch the initial cold shower water to refill the toilet tank or to water your garden with
* Catch the water that drains down from up in the showerhead after the shower is turned off
* Design your new home with the hot water heater closer to the bathrooms
* Don't clean your bathtub more than every two or three months
* Don't use soap scum remover
* Don't use drain cleaner. Clean your drains manually
* Don't flush the toilet if all you did was urinate in it
* Don't clean your home toilet with chemicals more than every five weeks
* Sani-Flush Toilet Bowl Cleaning Crystals will clean the toughest stains
* Place several water bottles into the bottom of your toilet tank to lower the amount per flush
* Take note of which workplace toilets flush with less water. There is a difference
* Use public toilets that have not yet been flushed
* Throw pet dung into the trash, not the toilet
* Ask for no-water urinals to be designed into your new home
* Design your home with two plumbing systems to capture and reuse gray shower water for flushing the toilets
* Design your home to have one composing toilet even if it's just for emergencies
* Look for top quality toilets like the *Champion* from American Standard that is a low maintenance/low flush toilet but that has a far more powerful flush despite using the same amount of water
* Washing your hands after just urinating is optional
* Turn the water off while soaping up your hands
* Only use cold water to wash your hands
* Just use a trickle to wet and rinse off
* Don't run the water to get a slightly colder drink
* Don't soak your dishes and glasses before washing. Wash them before things harden on
* Save the rinse water from last time in a pot and put small things to soak in there until the next time

- Use the rinse water from washing the initial dishes to soak the others. It only takes a few extra minutes
- Rinse out your glass and then simply drink the rinse water instead of dumping it down the drain
- Only use cold water to wash your dishes
- Washing your coffee cup—EVER—is optional
- Don't try to thaw out frozen meat by soaking it in water
- Simply reuse your glasses, plates and cooking pots without washing them if they don't look too bad
- Try to capture the rainwater from your roof to water your garden
- Washing and waxing your car is unnecessary apart from hosing off the road salt in the winter
- Don't wash your casual clothing any more than you would dry clean your suits
- Don't wash your bath towel every week. You only use it when you are perfectly clean
- Drink mostly water so as to avoid dehydration

Conserving Paper and Wood Products
- Recycle all paper products: remove staples, peal the labels off cans, the actual punch holes from a three-hole punch machine… whatever it takes!
- Buy more recycled paper products
- Save scrap paper instead of using sticky pads
- Use cloth napkins and dishrags
- Don't use paper towels in a public bathroom to dry your hands. Let your hands air dry
- Use a hanky instead of tissues
- Consider using used tissues as toilet paper
- Try to only use two to three sheets of toilet paper per wipe (eight to 12 sheets total per sitting)
- Use toilet paper made form recycled materials
- Pick up clean-looking napkins for your own use wherever you find them.
- Reuse your pizza box up to a half-dozen times then recycle the box
- Take your own bag to carry take-out orders in and when you go grocery shopping
- Only take one napkin at most from a restaurant and don't allow them to put so many in your takeout orders
- Try to reduce the number of bills you receive
- Use the duplex print option and try to lower your font and margin sizes
- Avoid wrapping Christmas presents and don't send birthday cards
- If you are given a paper plate and disposable utensils, save and reuse them
- A single roll of paper towels should last six months minimum

Not Wasting Food
- Always finish what you've taken
- Don't let leftovers sit
- Ask not what do I want to eat, but what needs to be eaten first so as not to spoil
- Eat more than your fill if food is going to go to waste
- It's ok to take the last portion of food rather than have it go to waste
- Eat the food that no one else wants
- Order the old pizza slices instead of the new. Hey, it's pizza!
- Buy food about to expire or that may be partially damaged
- Actually buy the carton of eggs with the broken egg in it so as not to have them throw away 11 good eggs
- Rearrange a store's shelf if food looks like it might fall off and break
- Consider licking your plate clean or using a bread role to wipe up any remaining crumbs
- Consider eating things that have fallen onto the floor
- Make George Costanza proud by eating food from the trash if it looks *alright*
- Vegetarianism saves on the food and water that the farm animals would have needed but may not be entirely healthy for many. To Native Americans, killing plants is no different than killing animals
- If you're a vegetarian, don't be afraid to eat meat if it's going to go to waste
- Cooking stew keeps all the nutrients within what you are going to eat and drink

- Decline dinner roles at a restaurant if you aren't going to eat them
- Ask for take out bags or—better yet—bring your own plastic containers
- Never return food just because it has a hair in it
- Avoid as many restaurants as possible as they waste a horrific amount of food and are equally wasteful to land

Saving Animals and Insects

- Apart from saving trees and rare mammals, our fight has to be for the insects as well
- Watch where you step and avoid stepping on any insect you can see
- Limit how much you walk on the grass and use the sidewalk instead
- Take longer steps when walking through the lawn
- Lower the amount you mow the lawn and try to use a non-motorized push mower
- Avoid even having a lawn to begin with and have a yard full of trees instead
- Check firewood for insect and simply toss the log to the side if they are living in it
- Carry a plastic baggy to capture insects trapped in areas where they won't be able to get out
- Don't use bug wackers, insecticides, or weed killer. They are devastating to everything that is out there including rabbits, ladybugs, worms, and spiders alike
- Try to use the hose or a pot of water to wash away pesky ants or insects first. They'll get the idea!
- Capture insects in your home with a clear glass and piece of paper in order to take them outside
- Don't be hateful. Killing 20, 30, or 300 gypsy moths isn't going to save the forest
- Don't be afraid to rescue insects form your toilet or your pet's water bowl
- Cover up open water sources that insects might accidentally land in
- Take even the smallest amount of bread or food crumbs outside for the insects
- Pick worms up off the road if they are likely to be run over
- Rescue pets from the street or the pound instead of buying special breeds
- Lower your travel at night when insects are more prone to be attracted to the headlights
- Don't crack your car windows in the summer to prevent insects from getting in
- Watch out for animals when you drive
- Drive the speed limit
- Carry heavy gloves in your car incase you have to move or rescue something
- Keep emergency animal hospital numbers in your wallet incase you hit a pet and the game commissioner's number incase you hit a deer
- DO NOT go out of your way to hit any animal with your car, not even a groundhog
- Groundhogs are awesome! Learn to love them just as much as the rarest of pandas
- Don't be afraid to stop your car and move a turtle to the side of the road. Grab them as far back as you can
- Road kill can sometimes be eaten if it's still fresh and is OVER cooked
- Road killed animals are a great source of animal hides, which can be made into the finest clothing
- Check your window wells for trapped frogs. It's not a good place for them
- Consider designing your home without window wells
- Do not build a home where it will impact a forest or trees

Handling Trash

- Carry a trash bag with you to pick up any recyclables you find
- Aluminum is the most valuable recyclable
- Please look out for and pick up nails, glass, or dead batteries
- Don't pick up cans or bottles with insects living in them
- Compost the hair from yourself (your electric razor included) and your pets
- Recycle aluminum foil (even from small candy) by placing it into an aluminum can
- Use shoes and clothing until they literally fall apart
- Report wastefulness at your workplace
- Pick up rubber bands before the sunlight degrades the rubber
- Don't be afraid to take recyclable bottles and cans out of the trash after a luncheon or at a park

- Don't throw away baby carriages or cribs. Give them to someone who needs them
- Donate old clothing to the Salvation Army

Saving Energy
- You can cook an entire one-pound box of spaghetti without even bringing the water to a full boil and without having any water to drain away at the end. Just heat the water and let it sit covered for 25 minutes
- Use the hot spaghetti to heat your spaghetti sauce
- Don't preheat your oven and try to turn it off several minutes before what you're cooking is done
- Take out all of the bathroom light bulbs except one and try to shower only by streetlight if possible
- Men might consider sitting at night to urinate in order to save on lighting
- Arrange home furniture to make use of natural lighting
- Buy OLED lights or long-life florescent bulbs in the meantime. You can save $55 over the life of the bulb
- Turn out the lights even at your workplace and in your workplace bathrooms
- Have your department maintenance personal remove excess florescent lighting from above your cube
- Design your new home so that the exhaust fan in the bathroom is not connected to the lighting
- Front-loading washing machines can use up to 60% less power
- Use fans instead of AC
- Avoid using AC below 84° or the heat above 64°
- Open and shut your refrigerator door quickly
- Keep your refrigerator full—even with emergency water—so that less air spills out when the door is opened
- Buy a refrigerator with a through-door opening so you can get select things without opening the entire door
- Let frozen food defrost on the counter before placing it into the microwave
- Eliminate excess TV time in favor of other activities like Yoga or sports
- Vacuum your home only once a month. Picking up stuff by hands can cut sweeper use to a third
- Don't leave the TV or a light on when you go out at night
- Don't use a hairdryer or electric toothbrush

Transportation
- Strategically pick places to live and live as close as you can to work
- Urban density is better than suburban sprawl, small towns included
- Hybrids are still too expensive. Buying the most basic economy cars is just fine
- Keep your vehicle until it falls apart
- Avoid sports cars, SUVs and luxury cars at all costs
- Learn the towing capacity of cars and minivans. It's often enough
- Buy hatchbacks or station wagons
- Do not warm up your car in winter or summer
- Don't change your oil excessively. I did mine every 10,000 miles
- Try to live without AC in your car in most areas
- If you own a standard shift, consider coasting your car down mountain sides and up exit ramps
- If buying more than one car, buy the same make and model so that you can interchange parts as they get old
- Walk or ride your bike to work
- Car pool
- Avoid driving as much as possible
- Plan trips to the store so that you hit multiple locations along the way
- Park your car a mile or so short of where you are going and simply walk the rest of the way
- Try taking public transportation one or two days a week if it's available

Conservation
- Don't use plastic wrap or aluminum foil
- Drink tap water to avoid wasting a plastic bottle
- Don't use Styrofoam cups

- Always use a reusable coffee cup
- Recycle even used staples
- When writing or drawing with pensile, write at a shallow angle and rotate the pensile to keep the point sharp
- Use erasers down to the 2 mm mark
- Plant more trees, up to ten billion nationwide
- Always foot the bill to repair an appliance (regardless of cost) instead of just buying a new one
- Hold off on buying the newest computers and gadgets until better models come out
- Use Consumer Reports magazine. Better products that last longer are more environmentally friendly
- Foot the bill for extra durable products that last, not cheap junk
- Are you sure you need an actual bed, or would a few camping mats do?
- Consider not having a phone or only a cell phone
- Pass up on freebee-offers if you don't need what they are giving away
- Avoid chemicals, all sorts of harsh cleaners, furniture polish, and most personal hygiene items
- Build communal or extended-family homes so that you can share appliances and vehicles with loved ones
- Learn to sew and make your own clothing
- **Always consider functionality before aesthetics**

10. *Fewer Wars and Smaller Military Budgets*

War is not a good economic policy, the ideal jobs program, or some sort of perverse method of population control. Using such myths and perverse reasons to justify warfare has allowed many to become all too comfortable with what essentially amounts to organized mass murder. Believing that war is somehow inevitable or perhaps even good, is indeed a dangerous path to tread in a world so utterly chockfull of **AAMD**s (Arsenals of Absolute Mass Destruction). Although some technical innovations are spurred by military development, such things can be equally derived from a more robust space program, extensive scientific research, and from within civilian industry itself.

Admittedly, a reasonable defense will be needed for the foreseeable future, but a single *Ohio-Class* ballistic missile submarine has the destructive force of **3,200** Hiroshima atomic bombs. Approximately sixteen of these submarines ply the waters of the world (among those of other nations) hoping to secure a favorable verdict in the world's final judgment. People think it's a dream, but we're literally crawling to just such an end, where the 'I' executes the 'me' in total Armageddon (Overkill - Horrorscope CD - Soulitude).

Machines and computers have made it easy to kill en masse. Sooner or later, someone is going to come to power and be hell-bent on using them. It isn't hard to imagine how criminals or extremists can worm their way into power or how generals might seize it outright. Austria, for example, elected a pro-Nazi politician who promised all sorts of false hopes a few years ago and even the U.S. and Japan have been engaging in more "nationalistic agendas" of late. As long as such exceedingly lethal militaries exist and are governed by nations that feel they can do no wrong, no one can honestly feel safe.

Warfare is not only extremely devastating, it is a horrific waste of much needed resources. To somehow avert it we must understand our own weaknesses. We must realize that things like blind nationalism and hatred are emotions (*not* religious attributes) that are all too easily provoked in our species regardless of race, religion, political background, or some perceived high standing. No one is immune! No nation can ever be fully assured that genocide will not happen within their borders or that its armies will not attempt to dominate the world by force. As it stands, we only think we are an advanced, god-fearing society.

However, we've yet to solve very many of the world's problems and are only creating that many more as we go. When will society decide to address its food, water, energy, education, healthcare, environmental, and housing concerns? Those are measures of how good a society is, not who has the biggest bombs and the most deadly stealth aircraft.

"We will either live together as brothers or die together as fools"
- Dr. Martin Luther King Jr. -

Thankfully, peace might actually be more possible in today's high-tech world than in times past. Advances such as international air travel, the Internet, global communications, and international engineering projects all help to build a global consciousness, cooperation, and a greater understanding for the diversity of cultures that exist. Space tourism might also help instill a greater sense of unity one day because of how changed astronauts report feeling after seeing the world from space.

Part of what is holding us back, however, is the fear that we are not secure and it is this same fear that is used to keep the masses subjugated and mistrustful of one another. So what could change this? With an international missile defense shield, WMD monitoring satellites, and a terror-proof transit system (that uses incredibly sensitive bomb detecting equipment and face recognition software), society could indeed be a little more clear-headed about its current situation. A battlefield laser defense system would allow countries like Israel to scoff at every rocket and mortar shell fired at them. Less dependency on foreign energy reserves and a greater self-sufficiency at the local-level would also eliminate potential points of international contention. Individually, if our homes were more secure, we'd have little to fear from gangs, militia groups, rioters, and natural disasters alike.

Other things that can help prevent wars would be to better equip our armies (with armored security vehicles) for peacekeeping duties and to establish a better international police force. This would enable us to separate warring factions (like in Bosnia and Iraq) long before ethnic and sectarian violence escalated into such widespread bloodshed, infrastructure damage, and the displacement of so many refugees. We could establish weapons-free zones around the world (as the Dalai Lama suggested) and even re-invent the U.N. to where no nation had veto abilities. Perhaps the U.N. should be organized like congress, where nations

---

Are Humans Inherently Peaceful or Violent?

Many people point to a history of warfare and crime and see humans as inherently violent. I think this assumption is false, however. If people are given good food, clothing, homes, jobs and income, they'll almost certainly be productive and peaceful members of society. Indeed, under normal, acceptable conditions, we are calm and cooperative beings. We love to help each other, we show up for work on time, and—as many 9/11 responders showed—we'll even die for each other! It's only when outside stresses are present (like finances or a repressive government) that cracks begin to show and violence emerges. Sure, there are some people with some serious issues and people can be both irritating and aggressive at times, but when things are going good and a respectable/unbiased police force is there to manage our outbreaks, we do quite well! In contrast, if humans were somehow inherently violent, then there would be no amount of comfort and no quite/calm environment that could ever change that.

have a number of representatives proportional to their population and economy. Perhaps the smallest possible self-governing states or—alternately—a world of just a few large superpowers will be the key to greater stability.

Overall, there is certainly hope. The European Union is itself proof that greater world peace and cooperation is possible under the right circumstances. Just look at how France and Germany—once sworn enemies during _two_ world wars—have become almost inseparable. Look at how countries like East Germany and Japan became productive members of society in just a few decades! As the European Union is fond of saying, *"You don't have to like your neighbor, you just have to trade with them."* In this sense, greater world trade is also leading to greater and greater spans of world peace. Going to war with each other has become almost impossible, as we'd literally have to shut down our own economies to do so.

Ultimately, there is just too much to gain when we work together. We live in a time where we can see the potential for a bright future with clean, limitless energy and a far greater standard of living for all. Events like Apollo 11 and 13 proved the world had but one heart, a heart that could indeed be engaged with the right spirit and challenge. Finding ways to engage it and keep it engaged will take sound leadership and a willingness to change. If we give in to hopelessness, however, almost nothing can or will be achieved. But if we all believe that we can make a difference and at least try, who knows what will happen?

Please note that a desire for peace is not—in any way—to suggest that we should lie down and be the victim of every crime. Protecting ourselves—and others—from harm is very much the best preventative measure we can employ. If we fail to do that, we ourselves become negligent of allowing bad things to happen. 9/11 is no different!

Those who are paranoid see criminals and threats in every shadow.
Those who are confident and have trained self-defense, look up from the shadows
to see a wonderful moonlit night!

- Chris Eldridge -

- The End -

SOURCE LISTING

Bruni, Frank. "Behind a Suburban Facade in Queens" The New York Times
        8 October 1996: B1+.

Communities Directory: A Guide to Cooperative Living. 2nd ed.
        Rutledge, Missouri: Fellowship for International Community (FIC), 1996.

Taisei Corporation: 1998 Annual Report. 2nd ed. 1-25-1 Nishi-Shinjuke, Shinjuku-ku,
        Tokyo 163-0606: Taisei Corporation, 1998.

 "All Things Considered [Census Bureau data on single-parent homes]" NCR
        Radio Broadcast. 18 September 1994.

Dubrin, Andrew J and R Duane Ireland. Management and Organization. 2nd ed.
        Cincinnati, Ohio: Southwester Publishing, 1993.

Brown, Terry & Linda, mainframe programmers. Personal Interview.
        29 October, 1998.

Angier, Bradford. Field Guide to Edible Wild Plants 15th ed.
        Harrisburg, PA: Stackplole Books: 1996.

Gail Cooper Allfirst Bank technical support. Personal Interview.
        June 2000.

Capra, Fritjof. Tao of Physics. 4th ed.
        Boston, MA: Shambhala: 1999.

Wasp. "Widowmaker." The Last Command.
        Blackie Lawless: 1985.

Judas Priest. "Blood Red Skies." Ram it Down.
        Glen Tipton, Rob Halford, and K.K. Downing: 1988.

Twin Oaks Visitors Liaison. Personal Interview.
        May 1999.

Stover, Dawn. "Canada's Advanced Houses." Popular Science
        March 1994: 73-77.

"Light Powers Antibacterial Tile." Popular Mechanics

Soviero, Marcelle M. "Concrete That Bends" Popular Science
        February 1991: 82.

Gorant, Jim. "Liquid Golf" Popular Mechanics
        July 1998: 30.

 "Computer Sees Through Disguises" Popular Mechanics
        June 1997: 22.

Cannon, Williams A. How to Cast Small Metal and Rubber Parts 2nd ed.
        New York, NY: Tab Books: 1986.

"Low-Cost Computer Prototyping" Popular Mechanics
        August 1997.

"Light Years [E-Lamps]" Popular Mechanics
        September 1992.

I would very much like to thank

Dio, Sabbath (incl. Martin and Gillan), Billy Squier, Ozzy, Purple, Rainbow, Priest (incl. Owens), Maiden (incl. Bayley), Savatage (incl. Stevens), Over Kill, W.A.S.P., Dickinson, Halford, Megadeth, fates warning, Queensryche, Metal Church, Heir Apparent, Chastain, Dee Snider, Lethal, Udo, and all of those in metal music, who put so much positive energy into their work that the universe, as we know it, will never be the same! Your pro-environment, antiwar, anti-drug, anti-corruption, and anti-pornography message was certainly something worth shouting about. The *self-belief* and gripping realism that your music imparted allowed me to believe in myself and that change was possible and indeed quite necessary.

Runs With Wolf: I stood up against the ways of the world with an unquestioned belief, but with few realistic chances of succeeding. Your acceptance of my early "estranged concepts" and willingness to pass these ideas on to your friends, gave me a tremendous goal to work for. I can't possibly thank you enough!

Carl Sagan's TV series *Cosmos* was about the only thing on this Earth that had the power to send me to college: proving on a personal level the value of science to inspire young people to want to learn. I am an avid reader of science material and review exoplanet counts almost daily. I sincerely hope that we will be able to fully read the history of our solar system in the next century or two. I'd love to see extensive orbiter and lander missions to the moons of Titan, Triton, and Europa! We aren't getting any younger.

Apart from Joy Matkowski, Tracy Skorka (PSU graduate and mainframe programmer), and Darrell Troutman, Karen Nitkem and my mom (Diane Smith—a former EDS programmer) have also been very helpful in reviewing many sections of this book!

Professor Bernard Williams—my English Composition II professor at one of the best community colleges on the planet—The Harrisburg Area Community College! Mr. Williams nurtured the initial stirrings of my writing skills on home design and was helpful in every way. Professor Cliff Dillmann and Terri Wallace also helped out on this difficult path!

I'd like to thank Alan Boyle of MSNBC's Cosmic Log for printing so many of my opinions. Having such a place where one's voice could be heard on such heartfelt issues helped me through several difficult periods. Each day became an opportunity I never had! *"Give a man a lever and a place to stand and he can move the world"* it's said…

I'd also like to thank Taoist, Buddhist, and Native American philosophies, which help to connect us with the subtleness of our diverse reality. The I Ching, the Te-Tao Ching, The Tao of Physics, and Insight Meditation, were books every bit as important in this journey.

Good luck all!

About the Author

Chris Eldridge earned an Associates Degree in mainframe computer programming at the Harrisburg Area Community College in 1997 and went on into a seven-year career in the field. While at college, he earned a 3.8 GPA and tutored programming and math.

Professional life never satisfied Chris, however. The activism instilled in him early on as a teen runaway and homeless person meant that he spent his personal time working to promote humanitarian and environmental progress: petitioning and protesting in every way he knew how. His first book, Conceptual Communal Home Design, aptly demonstrated a new and painstaking analytical approach to this *on and off again* way of life. His highly functional floor plans (developed over 19 years) systematically achieve a far higher quality of living for residents, while reducing land consumption 60% to 98%! The former governor of California, **Attorney General Jerry Brown,** commended Chris in writing for advocating such land-conscious designs.

Chris' second book—*Environmental Practices (7th ed.)*—documents the many things he learned about caring for the environment on a personal level, as well as how high technology has helped everything from oil tankers to jumbo-jet airliners become more environmentally friendly. The book also contains his latest home designs and a chapter on emergency preparedness.

Apart from his passion for designing, writing, science, history, and scrap-booking, Chris trained for eight years in the martial arts and for a few years in Tai Chi and yoga. He has studied Buddhism and Native American skills and has designed and sewn highly detailed outdoor clothing for himself for some 20 years. Chris authored a seven-page feature article for the magazine Law Enforcement Technology called *Preparing for a Super-Disaster* (8/04). He also had 38 pro-science and pro-peace reader-responses printed on MSNBC.com (and others) and is a member of the Jimmy Carter Center, which promotes peace, democratic values, and human rights worldwide.

Author Contact Information

For more information on this constantly evolving topic you can e-mail me at:

function_first@hotmail.com - or - function_first@verizon.net

or write:

Conceptual Communal Home Design/The Deliberacy...
Post Office Box 4314
Harrisburg, Pennsylvania 17111-0314

Environmental Practices: From Living Simply to Global Advancement (7th Ed.)

Environmentalism isn't just about global warming. There are many reasons to live more efficiently including for our health, the beauty of the natural world, an improved national security derived from energy independence, and for our own pocketbook. In the end, how can we ignore our part in ongoing environmental devastation thinking that all we need to do is recycle? Aren't wastefulness and carelessness morally wrong?

This full-size (8.25" x 10.75") book provides insightful hints that will help you lead a far more environmentally conscious lifestyle. Whether we use less water to shower with or drive an economy car, we must learn to question all of our actions to see if we are wasting things needlessly or can save still more. As such, there are chapters on conserving water, paper, food, energy, and consumables as well as on transportation and saving wildlife.

Apart from learning how to protect the environment on a personal level, there are chapters on high technology and how it's increasing the efficiency of our airliners, oil tankers, and semi-rigs. Some airliners, for example, will reduce CO2 emissions by 94% in the next two years alone! Understanding just how amazing our technology is gives us hope and helps us to see that this is <u>not</u> by any means a no-win situation.

"Environmental Practices offers creative ways, designs, and technology to protect and improve the state of our environment and I commend you for your comprehensive work…"
Senator Ted Kennedy (D-Mass)

Since super-disasters (or ultra-catastrophes) impact the environment just as much as our own society, there's a chapter on how our police and fire departments can better prepare for such events. With better emergency facilities, rescue helicopters, and vehicles, we'll be able to save more lives and respond to chemical and petroleum spills that much faster! Even the public can be better prepared with homes able to cope with live-in evacuees and minor storm damage.

The book's most extensive chapter is on modernized communal living. When done correctly, living communally can dramatically lower a society's environmental impact while still maintaining privacy and our standard-of-living. Such homes would have corporate telephone and server computer systems, segregated living areas, and master bedroom suites with full entertainment centers, personal computers, and <u>ample</u> storage space. There'd be wider hallways, soundproof materials within the walls and floors, and top-quality appliances to meet expected demands.

Most importantly, such homes would have professionally-equipped offices and shops that allow residents to establish comprehensive home-based businesses. Being able to work right from home lowers our impact on the environment and would allow highly skilled residents to launch an absolute renaissance in the quality of living that middle-class citizens can achieve. Craftsmanship would improve and more durable, commercial-quality homes could be built with the savings realized on travel-related expenses alone. Five conceptual home designs are presented along with this.

The book's final chapter touches on seven additional topics that can dramatically help the environment right <u>now</u>! They include the functionality of designs, product standardization, computerized traffic-control networks, and the need for smaller military budgets.

PLEASE NOTE: There are 52 pages of crossover between my books. Occasionally, one is more up-to-date than the other but one is likely all you need.

Printed in the United States
by Baker & Taylor Publisher Services